NEW WRITING SCOTLAND

NUMBER THREE

NEW WRITING SCOTLAND

3

Edited by
ALEXANDER SCOTT
and
JAMES AITCHISON

Managing Editor
DAVID HEWITT

Association for Scottish Literary Studies

Published by the
Association for Scottish Literary Studies
c/o The Department of English, University of Aberdeen
Aberdeen AB9 2UB

First published 1985

ISBN 0 9502629 6 X

The Association for Scottish Literary Studies acknowledges
with gratitude subsidy from the Scottish Arts Council
in the publication of this volume

Printed by AUP Aberdeen

CONTENTS

INTRODUCTION

New Writing Scotland 3, like the first two volumes in the series, has attracted work by new writers who have published little or nothing before now and yet have a remarkable maturity and confidence of voice as well as impressive technical skills. And the *New Writing Scotland* series is now attracting a growing number of more experienced writers who see the anthology as an important outlet for their new work.

No writing in Gaelic and very little in Scots was submitted for this issue of the anthology, and we are left with the impression that writers in these languages are looking to the specialist magazines for publication. There is too the impression that although younger generations of Scottish writers readily use local dialect in their fiction or poetry, they seldom write an entire work either in dialect or a more literary form of Scots. One result of this may be that part of Scotland's story, the story of some of its people, is not being told.

In fiction we find that the main concern this year as in previous years is the integrity of the individual, and at the centre of several of the short stories there are personal dilemmas, domestic crises, interrupted relationships. People are examined with a scrupulous intimacy, a proper balance of inquisitorial rigour and sensitivity that leads to some rewarding insights. When the writers explore the extremes of experience — exile, illness, violent death —they do so in finely controlled, subtly understated narratives.

The main feature of the poetry this year is probably its diversity. There are few signs of the petty tyrannies of poetic fashion or fashionable preoccupations. Instead, there is a wide variety of subject matter, an unassuming originality of treatment, and a willingness to explore public issues as well as personal experience with an independent and sometimes refreshingly subversive vision.

Alexander Scott
James Aitchison

Glasgow, 1985

GILLEAN SOMERVILLE

AU BAR MAROC

The old man wove his way between the tables, café after café, down the broad busy street. He wore a white crocheted skull cap, a dusty black jacket, white vest, cream-coloured cotton trousers and had a large leather purse slung across his chest. He was selling brown and white striped blankets, the cheap version of the Berber one she had bought for George in the native quarter that afternoon, rich with greasy, but allegedly authentic, fibres of lamb and camel and dromedary. She bent her head to her postcards in the hope that he would pass her by.

She might have expected otherwise. 'The thing about the Arabs,' she could hear George saying, 'is that when they want something they just pitch their tents and wait.' She had to look up eventually. Mutely, the old man's grizzled face twisted itself into an appeal, one arm holding out a blanket for her inspection. He had come too late, however. A day of dodging similar, if more articulate appeals made her momentarily hard. She shook her head firmly and returned her attention to her postcards. When she next looked up it was to find, somewhat to her surprise, that he was gone. Her eyes followed him as he shambled on down the street. He was tired, perhaps, at the end of a long day, not up to the hassle of trying to persuade one lonely British lady tourist who did not speak his language and who probably knew her own mind.

She felt sorry for him and guilt for refusing him. A few more pounds might have made his day and wouldn't have torn a hole in her bank balance. And she would have had the blanket as a souvenir of her charity. One of the primary tenets of Islam enjoined giving alms to the poor. But one could not give to all. In the narrow crowded streets of the native quarter that morning they had been besieged by children, thin and agile, darting about, some with babies on their backs, shouting at them, *'Un dirham, s'il vous plaît, madame. Monsieur, un dirham, s'il vous plaît. Bonbons! Cigarettes!'* Some of the adults would reprimand the children, but to no avail. They simply reappeared elsewhere. She noticed how their guide,

Mujid, only gave coins to the old people who sat with silent patience in the shade of the walls outside the mosque. The children he brushed off like insects.

She signalled to the elderly white-jacketed waiter and asked him for some more mint tea. 'This is a mendacious city,' she had written to George, 'but then I am only seeing it from a tourist's point of view.' Her eyes took in two young Arabs at a neighbouring table who were evidently sizing her up. Good Heavens, at *her* age! On the other hand, it wouldn't be the first time that day. Her eyes swept over them. She supposed that if she had simply come to this country for casual sex she would not have had any difficulty. The complete inaccessibility of their own women led to all sorts of presumptive and irritating expectations. Oh, she might as well relax and be flattered. George was a dead loss in that department these days.

The mint tea arrived. She lit a cigarette and leaned back in her chair. What a relief to be on her own again for an hour or two. It had been a tiring day. All four days of the trip so far had been tiring. The first night in the grubby campsite in Malaga, disturbed by the scratchings of famished cats rooting among the rubbish bins outside their tents. The dawn dash to Algeciras, the charm of the coast overshadowed by the soaring concrete jungles of holiday apartments, many still unfinished. Long hold-ups at ferry and frontier among crowds of homing Moroccans, their cars piled high with treasures earned in Europe, the pleasurable compensations of menial work and low wages. Overnight they had camped off the road north of Tetuan, waking in the morning to the sight of storks perched on a nearby crenellated rooftop and the stares of silent children herding goats who hid as soon as they took out their cameras. And yet, with all the fatigue there had been magic too. Their first sight of the northernmost hills of Africa looming up through the blue heat haze that veiled the Straits. A peasant woman riding to market on her donkey along the untrafficked ribbon of road from Tetuan to Chechuan, her head shaded by her broad-brimmed hat trimmed with strands of dark blue wool. A water wheel by a bridge. Sellers of prickly pears by the roadside, the fruit on the bushes reminding her of human feet. Huge ungainly hemp plants leaning over the road like bands of triffids on the march. Then the arches of the old Roman city rising from the flat and fertile plain, its empty streets, the ruins of its villas, forum, seat of government and the temples of its gods. And

now they had come to this city, with its ancient Islamic traditions and its modern commercial energy.

The others had left at six for a special meal and floor
show to make up for the disappointing meal they had had
the evening before; all except two young girls upstairs in the
hotel who were starving the spasmodic diarrhoea out of their
systems, the first casualties of the trip, and an elderly Aust-
ralian who was missing his wife and had gone to bed early.
She had waved goodbye to the truck as it lurched its way up
the street, its occupants crammed together but waving cheerfully, washed and eased into carefully preserved smart cotton
clothes after the hot and dusty day tramping around in shorts
and bush hats. Another time she might have envied them, but
just then she was glad to escape the claustrophobic conformity
of the truck and the stereotyped packaging masquerading
under the pretence of 'a more adventurous holiday.'

She watched the passers-by. Apart from a preponderance
of Arab features and the leavening of skull-caps, djellabahs,
kaftans and veils, it could have been a busy town in the south
of France, territory with which she was more familiar. Then,
suddenly, over the bustle of people and the hum of traffic,
came the long slow bellow of the *muezzin*. Before leaving
London she had looked forward to hearing it. 'It'll make a
change from church bells,' she had said to George. She was
surprised at how little she liked it. Invading her sleep at dawn
that morning, it had depressed her with its harsh, dry, un-
earthly sound. She had pulled the pillow over her head to try
to drown it out, but its message was not to be denied. The
loud, insistent monotone made her shiver. Its effect was
muted this evening. No one seemed to be taking much notice.
As in secular Europe, life went on regardless, it seemed. Perhaps it would help if one could make sense of the words.
'*Allah Akhbar*. There is no God but God and Mohammed is
His Prophet.' Strange how Moslems and Christians had this
mirror image of each other as Unbelievers.

Turning sideways, she observed three men from the hotel
— the receptionist, the bar manager and one of the waiters —
seated on the threshold, equally absorbed in the passing scene.
Business wasn't brisk just then, apparently.

'Postcards, *madame*, postcards! *Bonsoir, madame*. I am
from Mujid. I recognise you. I saw you this afternoon in the
medina with Mujid and all the other English tourists from the
truck. Mujid send me with postcards.'

Clearly to be left on one's own was not the prerogative of

a tourist in this country. He was a bright attractive boy.
About fifteen, perhaps? Articulate, well-educated, good English. Being groomed up by Mujid in his school holidays presumably. Mujid probably had a stable of boys like this, eager
to regard tourists as fair game for their pocket money.
    'You see this picture, *madame*? That is the *Place Ned-
jarine* where I saw you this afternoon.'
    'Did you really?'
    He nodded vigorously.
    There was something a little unnerving in the idea of
being observed like that, like being marked down and caught
in the sights of a hunter's gun. However, she did want some
postcards. She took the proferred bundle in her hand. The
boy sat down beside her. The views were good, although the
detail of the intricate carving inside the *medrasa* was dis-
appointingly blurred.
    'How much?'
    'Ten for ten dirhams, *madame*.'
    Twenty pence for a postcard? She shook her head.
    'Too much.'
    'Oh, no, *madame*. Look at the quality. Look at this one
of the mosque, madame. And this one of the shrine of the
Moulay Idriss. No, ten for ten dirhams, madame. Fixed price.'
    Fixed price. That was probably the fashionable gambit.
Fixed price absurdly high. All day it had been the same. All
day they had been subjected to badgering and bargaining,
chivvying and cajoling, in a variety of modes from the arrog-
antly contemptuous to the languidly charming. That rug she
had brought, richly patterned in red and blue and green.
Style Rabat. Quality extra-superior. Price exorbitant. It was
made by a women's co-operative, they had been told, each of
whom was paid six dirhams a day. 'A piece of Moroccan art,'
said Mujid, twirling his moustache, 'to remember when all
your other cheap souvenirs are forgotten and thrown away.'
She suspected that the women rug-makers wouldn't see much
of her money. Who then would? Omar, possibly, the swag-
gering master of ceremonies, with his jokes fit only for the
ears of Texan oilmen or Australians from the outback. Or
Mujid, in his sparkling white kaftan, calculating his com-
mission on the miniature electronic calculator built into his
wristwatch? The silent servers bringing mint tea? The sharp-
featured woman writing out the invoice? Certainly not the
men who had finally parcelled up the rug. Their labour had
been extra.

Faced with the undoubted skill of these Arab bargainers, she had little strength, or even will, to resist. Bargaining took time. Moreover, you needed to know the relative worth of what you wanted to buy. There were rough rules of thumb. Bid one third of the asking price. Bid what you feel something is worth to you. Elias Canetti, in his book, *The Voices of Marrakesh*, which she had brought with her to read on the trip, said that the real price of anything remained the secret of the seller. The asking price could vary according to the time of day or who you were. Generally the rich did better than the poor. 'Trust me and I get you very good price.' 'Madame, you raise your price a little, I lower mine and then we agree.' There were many such refrains. The most successful bargainer on the truck was a deaf and dumb boy, an apprentice carpenter. She suspected that the Arabs were compassionate towards him on account of his disability.

She chose ten cards and opened her handbag.

'You seem an intelligent boy. Are you at school?'

'Yes, madame.'

'What are you studying?'

'*Science* and *mathématique*. To be an *ingénieur*.'

'I'm sure you're very ingenious.'

She gave him the ten dirhams he asked for. From his dismissive reaction and abrupt departure she realised she had not earned respect. She had capitulated too soon. She shrugged. It was only a few postcards, for Heaven's sake. Moreover, what did she expect of a commercial transaction? The boy had his money. He had won. She was a tourist and a woman of mature years. Of no possible interest to a young boy. Yet, irrationally, it hurt her pride.

'Excuse me, *madame*?'

Oh, no, not another interruption. She looked up. It was Aziz, the bar manager from the hotel, and the waiter she recognised as having served them breakfast that morning.

'Excuse me for interrupting you, *madame*, but what time do you have breakfast tomorrow morning? The drivers from the truck have not told me and I have to tell Hassan before he goes home tonight.'

She hesitated.

'I think we leave at seven,' she said, unwilling to suggest too early a time. The drivers were always whipping them up at six for the long day's driving ahead. She would have liked to sabotage this tendency if she could.

The two men spoke in Arabic. Hassan departed. Aziz

hovered. He has a nice face, she thought.

'I'm enjoying this mint tea,' she said.

He bowed.

'Thank you very much. But why you not come down into my bar in the hotel and I make you mint tea there?'

Aziz's bar was in the basement, in a corner of the restaurant where they had breakfast.

She gestured to the street.

'I wanted to watch the people passing by.'

'But is dark now. Most people go home. There is less to see.'

'True,' she acknowledged. 'But in a foreign country even the most ordinary things are new and interesting to a stranger.'

He waited, a little hesitant.

'Tell me,' she went on. 'Is there anywhere I can buy stamps just now?'

'Stamps? No problem. Come with me. Is just down the street.'

She picked up her postcards, her copy of Canetti and the notebook in which she had intended to keep a diary of the trip, but in which so far she had barely written a line, and followed him. Aziz led her into a small stationer's shop and spoke to the elderly djellabahed man inside in Arabic.

'What you want exactly?' he asked her.

'Four stamps for postcards to Great Britain'.

Aziz conveyed her requirements. The old man produced the stamps. Aziz told her the price. She paid. Aziz seemed to insist on something to the old man. The stamps disappeared and were then handed to her in an envelope.

'Very nice stamps,' said Aziz, patting the envelope. 'Special issue to celebrate our king and his father.'

'Thank you.'

'Now you come and speak with me in my bar?'

'Well, ... '

She looked at her watch.

'I have to go to bed early. We have to get up very early in the morning and I am very tired.'

An anxious crease seamed his forehead.

'But I want to speak with you. I have wanted to speak with you since you arrive at the hotel, but always you push me away.'

She looked at him in genuine astonishment.

'Did I really?'

He nodded.

'Perhaps you don't remember?'

'If I appeared rude, then I'm very sorry. I did not intend ...'

'Is all right now. You come and speak with me in my bar?' Oh, why not? He wasn't offering her anything she couldn't handle. Besides, why *had* she come to this country? To view the landscape and places of interest. To absorb the atmosphere of the towns and villages and the markets where they bought their food. To examine the craftwork and buy souvenirs. But to speak to anyone? — other than asking directions and making simple purchases.

'All right then. For a little while.'

As she allowed him to lead her downstairs she had a distinct sense of crossing a frontier, of propelling herself through an inhibition she had not realised she possessed. Till now she had merely been an onlooker in this country, a traveller passing through. This man had made her feel ungracious, a characteristic she only normally displayed under provocation. Aziz had not provoked her, as Omar had, as George often did. Simply and politely, he had sought to engage her attention. She followed him.

The truck left at seven the following morning. She didn't hear the *muezzin* at dawn and her room-mate had to shake her awake at a quarter past six. She drank her coffee in a sleepy haze and asked the waiter if he could bring her a bottle of mineral water for the journey.

'*L'épicier est fermé a cette heure,*' he said, looking at his watch.

'*Mais derrière le bar?*'

He foraged behind the bar counter and eventually emerged with a cool litre bottle of Sidi Harazem.

'*Madame, cette bouteille est gratuite,*' he said, handing it to her with a smile and a flourish.

'Well, I say!' laughed her room-mate. 'What did you get up to, then, all on your own last night?'

Barbara grinned happily, but said nothing. It was her secret after all.

For the next few days their route was due south and then west. There was much to absorb them in spite of the heat and the dust and their chronic fatigue and each new unheralded bout of vomiting and diarrhoea.

The desert region took them by surprise. Not sand, but

stones. Later George, examining her slides, was to say, 'My
God, it looks like the sort of country where no one in their
sane senses would want to go.' But at the time it had not felt
like that. High canyons of magenta and apricot earth, tall
pillars of weathered stone, wide flat wastes of gravel dotted
with tumbleweed, fortress towns flying the red flag with its
green 5-point star, moslem cemeteries like vegetable gardens
but sown with stones, oasis towns blossoming out of the dryness, fringing some fertile river bed and flagged with date
palms. Old men in white turbans and pale djellabahs riding by
on donkeys would rein in their animals and stare. So would
the women, carrying their waterpots on their heads along the
dusty margin of the road, all but their eyes concealed beneath
their black cotton veils, on which the rich embroidery shone
like flames.

Eventually the earth turned black, the stones heaped up
like slates. They bought fossils, apparently gathered, smoothed
and polished by the people living in the meagre habitations of
that inhospitable expanse. Speaking no European language,
they communicated by signs, indicating how much they
wanted. Barbara had a tough time with a toothless old Arab
in a turban who wasn't prepared to part with his treasure for
a song.

There was a water stop by some sand dunes, almost the
only sand they saw and its burning surface roasted their feet.
Afterwards they bathed in a large water tank behind a small
bar advertising Pepsi and Seven Up.

'*Ici*,' a boy from the bar said, '*on n'a pas eu de la pluie
depuis quatre ans.*'

'*Et comment vivent les gens d'ici?*' Barbara asked.
'*Qu'est-ce qu'ils font pour gagner la vie?*'

He seemed momentarily puzzled by the question. She
had tried to keep the incomprehension out of her tone, but
perhaps she had failed. How do people live here? How *can*
they?

'*Maintenant ils partent pour les villes,*' he answered at last.

At another well they stopped to photograph a herd of
camels drinking. The camel-driver, effervescent with curiosity,
climbed up the outside of the truck and leaned in, grinning
with wordless curiosity.

In the towns they bargained for embroidered veils and
Berber jewellery, woven camel-bags and curved silver daggers
and bought fresh mint to brew up as tea with their evening
meals in camp.

The nights were the best part, fractionally cooler than the days. They would lie on top of their sleeping-bags under the glittering stars and marvel at their clarity and the silence.

'No wonder the Arabs were the first great astronomers,' said someone.

'It's what's happened to them since then that fascinates me. Like ancient Greece and Persia. What's happened to all that civilisation?'

'I put it down to their religion. Islam doesn't do much to encourage anyone's initiative.'

Dear George, You were right, of course. You wouldn't have liked it here. Tonight we're in Zagora. I'm lying under a ripening date palm. On my right is a hedge of pomegranate bushes bursting with fruit. It might be paradise on earth if it weren't for the flies and the heat and the cockroaches in the campsite loo. You know my fastidiousness about these things. Every time I say, 'Never again' and yet here I am. It draws me, this country. I can't say why. Love, Barbara.

My dear Aziz, Many thanks for the bottle of mineral water which Hassan gave me for breakfast. Everyone was very impressed and curious, of course. Yesterday we climbed the Tizi'n Test Pass into the High Atlas. I've never seen anything so spectacular. Today we arrived in Marrakesh. So far I haven't been ill, although almost everyone else has. I like your country very much. If only we had more time or could stop being tourists. I think of the cool privacy of Arab homes and gardens which the tourists never see. Love Barbara.

At first his very Arabness had frightened her. Although she had idly noticed that many of the young men were handsome, she was not attracted to their dark semitic looks. She had not really wanted to talk to Aziz. It was nothing personal. Just fatigue and a need for space and time. What could come of it, after all? More than anything, she hadn't wanted another Omar.

Omar had been the master of ceremonies in the carpet emporium in the native quarter where she had bought her rug. Slightly overweight but sleek, like a well-fed tom-cat, in his slim cut French cotton shirt, he had made her gorge rise with his vulgarity. Most of the other women felt the same. She had bought her rug nevertheless and was descending the stairs after signing the cheque for it when Omar had seized her arm and pulled her with him into a small ante-room with a divan right round the walls, out of sight of the rest of the group. Taken by surprise, she had found no strength to resist and sat uneasily, her rolled up rug perched on her knee.

'Tell me,' he began, with a well-practised air, 'has anyone ever told you that you have a beautiful body?'

Did he suppose that no one ever had? George had been reasonably complimentary, she recalled, until she had started putting on weight again.

'Oh no, I'm far too fat. British men don't like fat women.'

What an asinine response. He nodded sagely, as if this were a common factor among the women he propositioned. Perhaps it was.

'I understand. But, you see, the Arab, he like a woman with some flesh.' His hands reflected his words. 'Skin and bone, that is not interesting. Tell me, what are you doing this evening?'

She explained that there was a meal arranged. The following morning they had an early start.

'Besides, this is no part of the deal.'

'What deal?'

She pointed to the rug on her knee.

He regarded her purchase with contempt.

'There is no deal.'

She shrugged.

'You mean,' he went on, his voice rising steadily with his incomprehension, 'you are refusing what could be the best experience of your trip to Morocco?'

'I'm afraid so.' How else could one deflate such arrogance?

He looked at her in disbelief.

'Perhaps I see you this evening then?'

'Perhaps.'

He let her go. When she rejoined the group she found that she was shaking.

'I don't want to speak to tourists,' Aziz was saying. 'I want to speak to *you*'.

'But I *am* a tourist.'

'No, no. Tourists are not interesting. They come, they go, they see nothing. They cannot speak the language. They are not interested in the culture.'

'It is very hard for tourists,' she replied. 'Sometimes they do try to understand — some of them at any rate. But a holiday is over very quickly and the rest of the year they have to work very hard to pay for it.'

Aziz grimaced and changed the subject.

'You speak very good French. Where did you learn it?'

'In Marseilles, I suppose. I spent a year there as an *assistante* in a *lycée* when I was a student. I was studying French and had to spend a year abroad as part of my degree. I teach French, you see.'

He nodded.

'I worked in Nîmes,' he said. 'You know it?'

'But, of course. I got to know that part of France very well when I was living there.'

Ancient memories of Claude and the battered 2CV. Like looking through the wrong end of a telescope. So distant and almost forgotten now. He had done his national service in Algeria. He hadn't liked the Arabs much, she remembered. Like many French people.

'This is your first time in Morocco?'

Was it wise to admit so much?

'Yes,' she said.

'Why learn Arabic, for God's sake?' asked George several weeks later when she had returned home.

'Why not? A great many people speak it.'

'But when would you use it? You don't intend to go back there, surely? And what literature is there to speak of? You'd be better off with Russian.'

'Come the prospective Holocaust, you mean?'

'Think of the literature.'

'And how long do you suppose it would take me to learn enough to read Dostoievsky in the original?'

'Well, you managed Flaubert and Balzac and Zola.'

It was a stubborn name, George. Just like the man. Pipe and sports jacket. Armchair sport, armchair politics and the poetry of Hugh MacDiarmid.

'I don't understand,' he went on, 'what so many women find so fascinating about the bloody Arabs. They treat their women like dirt.'

'Don't be misled,' she retorted. 'In my experience there's no race on earth that treats its women well.'

'I would like to sleep with you,' said Aziz, 'but if you do not want to, is okay.'

Expressing herself honoured, she declined politely. The problem was, she said, that European women weren't always in pursuit of sex.

'But I,' said Aziz, sweeping into the attack, 'I have been exploited by European girls. They have come to hotels where I work and all they are interested in is to fuck. Is true. Has happened to me often. Once there was a Portuguese girl. I go to bed with her one night. The next night I look for her in my bar. She is there with someone else. Every night with someone different. If is all you want, then okay, is easy. But if I make love with you, I want to be close to you, to know you, to spend time with you. You understand me?'

She nodded. This wasn't like Omar, or was it just more skilful?

'Is a pity you go away tomorrow,' he went on. 'I would like to take you out, to show you my city, to meet my family. I have a nice family. Will you come out with me tonight when I finish my work?'

She shook her head.

Almost brusquely, he tried another tack.

'When do you come back to Morocco?'

He spoke as if it were a foregone conclusion.

'Oh, I don't know. Next year, perhaps.'

'Is all right. I can wait.'

My dear Aziz, It is already autumn here. The leaves on the trees have turned brown and gold. For a little while it's glorious, as if the woods are on fire. But then the leaves wither and the trees are bare and the rain falls and before you know it winter's here. Autumn reminds me that I'm getting older. I see from the newspaper that the temperature in Casablanca is still 24 degrees. I expect you're all still going about in shirt-sleeves.

She hadn't found him particularly handsome. That wasn't what had drawn her to him. He wasn't young, not much younger than herself. His manner was a trifle nervous and abrupt. Perhaps he had disarmed her by defeating her expectations of a conventional pick-up. Perhaps it was not so much the man himself as something beyond him, something she craved beyond the physical, beyond the individual, something associative in the austere white lines and moulded domes of his religion.

And then later, travelling through the desolate wastes on the margins of the Sahara, she had come face to face with the dryness of her own life, how cramped her spirit, how perished her imagination, and like those nomadic people they encountered, with their scraggy camels and their folding black tents, forever, as if purposelessly, on the move, she had no idea how she might escape.

'What is your name?' asked Aziz.
'Barbara.'
'Barbara?' He tried it on his tongue once or twice. 'Is like our "Berber".'
'It probably has the same origin. The Romans saw the native north Africans as a barbaric people, wild and uncivilised.'
'No. Is nice name. Barbara.'
'Having lived with it all my life, I don't think much of it.'
'Then I will give you an Arab name. We have nice names for women, paying them compliments. Also men.'
'What does your name mean?'
'Aziz, it means "Beloved".'
'How very nice.'
'Yes, my family they love me very much.'
I wish I could say the same, thought Barbara.

'Why do you think we should learn foreign languages?' she asked her first year, again as enthusiastic as ever to learn and to show off.
'Please, miss, so that when you're on your holidays in a foreign country you can ask for things you want.'
'Please, miss, so that you can talk to people from foreign countries who don't speak English.'
'Please, miss, so that you can listen in to foreign radio stations and pick up news of wars and killings and things like that.'
They were familiar, this generation, with global terrorism and unrest.
'Please, miss, because if people understand other languages it might bring them together and understand each other better and perhaps there wouldn't be any more wars.'
'Please, miss, so that you can read poetry and watch plays in the original language.'
Always the grand aspirations. And then the homely anecdotes.
'We were in Barcelona this summer and my dad speaks Spanish ... '
'My sister's studying Russian at unviersity and she says

. . . ,'

She liked, however, to provoke them to think.
'Do you think we can communicate without words?'
That usually stumped them. So she got them to improvise.
That was fun. And then they got down to the serious business of the session.

By comparison, the sixth form were jaded and cynical. A small, select group, all destined for university, they were pale with examination effort and unrealised expectations of love. Realising that she represented unfulfilment in their eyes, she liked to send little shock waves through their mock sophistication.

'You have to remember, when all's said and done, that the ultimate purpose of learning foreign languages for most people is for buying and selling. Secrets, sex and souvenirs. The language of the spy, the businessman and the tourist. How many English people, do you suppose, read *War and Peace* in the original Russian, let alone *The Qu'ran* in the original Arabic?'

They were suitably silent, as befitted those who had for months been battling their way, with copious commentary from edited critiques and from herself, through *La Princesse de Clèves, Phèdre, Candide, Madame Bovary, La Nausée* and *L'Etranger*. The one text they really felt they understood and were never tired of discussing, *Le Deuxième Sexe*, they had all read in English.

'What is the point of what we're doing then?' asked Cecily Houlston, with her customary little-girl-lost look. Reckoned academically to be the weakest of the group, she was a girl, Barbara noted with interest, who had a good grasp of the system in which they all functioned.

'That sounds a good theme for an essay,' said Barbara. 'The benefits and drawbacks of a cultural education.'

Chorus of groans. 'You can't *do* this to us, Miss Thomson!'

'Come, come. Some critical self-awareness will do you no harm.'

'Production line culture, Miss Thomson,' said Joanna Rushborne, the cleverest of the group. 'Rows and rows of conscientious little robots being programmed with correct opinions on Racine and Flaubert ready to be delivered at the press of the examination button.'

'Well, that's one view, Joanna. I want some well-balanced thinking, please. A five paragraph plan by Friday.'

'Just what I meant,' drawled Joanna, as reluctant hands stretched out for well-thumbed notebooks to record the requirement.

'Please, Miss Thomson, they do say, don't they, that if you want to learn a language really well, the best thing to do is to take a lover. What do *you* think?'

'They could be right Cecily. The problem with lovers, however, is that they tend to unbalance the mind.'

Grins and knowing looks.

'Do you know that, statistically, ninety-two per cent of marriages between Moslems and Christians end in divorce?'

Barbara hadn't been sure that her university philosopher friend, Zita, was the wisest person to confide in. George was no use and Zita, in contrast to all her married friends with their family preoccupations, seemed the most alertly up to date and to have the most varied experience of life to draw on. But Zita at thirty-nine was beginning to show her age, Barbara felt. Her zeal for experiment seemed to have died. Her intellect was sharper than her feelings. She was more concerned with lobbying for promotion than with dropping out. Her features were beginning to look pinched, too, the result of vegetarianism and aerobics as much as of rational thought. She still dressed with her usual shabby flamboyance in multi-coloured smocklike Afghan dresses and wore dangly gilt earrings shaped like crescent moons. Barbara had always suspected that deep down Zita had difficulty reconciling the earth mother with the scholar. One must choose, Zita had said, and having chosen stick with one's choice.

'Is that so?' asked Barbara. 'Where did you get hold of a fact like that?'

Zita's reply was oblique.

'I nearly married an Arab once.'

'Really? You never told me!'

'My dear Barbara, the occasion never arose. Besides, it's not an episode I'm particularly proud of.'

'Why not?'

'Oh, I was green and silly, I suppose. Wildly romantic. We were both of us following courses at the Sorbonne. He was dark and handsome and quite delicious in bed and I thought I was being fearfully daring. The wilder shores of love and all that.'

'What happened?'

'Fear in the end. I discovered another woman. I also read

some books on Islam and didn't take to the Prophet's view of women. Then there was the extended family in Marrakesh requiring indefinite subsidy. I always seemed to be lending money against an infinitely receding day of reckoning. I'm essentially a capitalist individualist. That's why I've stayed single, let alone not married a Moslem.'

'Morroco's hardly Saudi Arabia.'

'My dear child, just be warned. The European veneer's pretty thin.'

Zita lit another Balkan Sobranie and topped up their glasses with the dry white Mosel wine which she now ordered by the case.

Late the following September, a week or so after the school had resumed for the new session, Cecily Houlston, whose colloquial French had improved by leaps and bounds over the summer, arrived in the school secretary's office to ask if there would be any possibility of Oxbridge tuition till Christmas.

'Hmm.' Miss Grayling fixed her with a stare and then removed her spectacles, letting them hang across her substantial bosom, suspended from her neck by a thin leather strap. 'You're one of Miss Thomson's "bairns", are you not?'

An old girl of the school, Miss Grayling carried herself like a duchess. This aroused ambivalent reactions in visitors unused to the traditions of the school and expecting secretaries to know their place. The girls understood her, however. Cecily nodded.

'Then you'll have to speak to Miss Wiseman first, I'm afraid. I'll just see if she's available.'

The intercom crackled.

'Miss Wiseman will see you now. Just go straight in.'

Miss Wiseman was a tall, thin, commanding lady, permanently robed in her academic gown. While she automatically drew awe from the girls, an adult would have discerned a shyness incompletely masked. 'Neither man nor woman, but a participant of both sexes,' Joanna Rushborne had surmised. To all of them she was a phenomenon, all that their mothers were not and a role model none of them would have dared wish to emulate.

'Well, Cecily, how nice to see you again at last. I trust that you have benefited from, as well as enjoyed, your sojourn in the south of France?'

'Oh, yes, Miss Wiseman, thank you.'

She couldn't find the words to apologise for her late return, let alone explain it. She felt untimely ripped as it was
from those nights of honeyed passion in the barn with Jean-
Paul. Only his imperative return to Paris had brought it to an
end. But Miss Wiseman, simply by looking at her in that steady
way she had, seemed to surmise it all.

'You have a good healthy colour, at any rate. The sun has
been kind to you.'

Cecily twitched but glowed all the same.

'Which brings me to another matter on which the sun has
apparently shone.'

Cecily prepared to look attentive.

'The universities must be used to our sending them young
women with perfect *argot* and a somewhat less than perfect
prose style. A feature of Miss Thomson's teaching for upwards
of twelve years now. But you do us credit in the end. Always
a good crop of firsts.'

Cecily smiled agreeably. She was not hopeful of Honours.
She had always been told not to raise her sights too high.

'However, this year, Cecily, you find us in an unexpected
dilemma. You haven't heard, I take it, that Miss Thomson has
left us?'

'No?'

'When I returned from Rhodes with Miss Pritchard on the
twenty-ninth of August there was a letter waiting for me. Air
mail, from an unspecified address in North Africa. Miss
Thomson had clearly intended to give me at least a month's
notice. In fact, I had ten days.'

'What's happened to her?'

'She has married, it seems.'

'Gosh! An oil sheikh or something?'

'An Arab certainly. A Moroccan apparently. He works in
a hotel, she says. Oil sheikhs, I understand, inhabit the Gulf
region.'

'Wow!'

'Yes, Cecily, your surprise is the equal of my own. Miss
Thomson was of an age and educational attainments beyond
such foolishness. How premeditated it was, I have no means
of knowing. She was in Morocco last year too. She may have
met him then. She expresses her apologies to any of you who
come back hoping for Oxbridge tuition. Miss Markworth
lacks experience, I'm afraid. I have had to buy in help from a
retired teacher, a Miss Pettigrew, until a permanent appointment is made. All very unprofessional and utterly unexpected.

Miss Thomson was always so reliable.'

Was there a trace of jealousy in Miss Wiseman's tone? Was there any need to have given away so much?

'I could go back to Aix,' said Cecily. 'There's a family I can stay with and I can study at the university. They have lots of courses for foreigners.'

'That's all very well, my dear, but you mustn't neglect your texts. They are what you will be examined on, after all.'

The telephone wires hummed, the letters fairly buzzed with the news as it spread among the girls.

'Heavens, she must be nearly *forty* if she's a day! The Arabs can't be very particular!'

'I think it's perfectly *lovely*! She was quite attractive really! I can't understand why someone didn't carry her off years ago! I always thought it was a tragedy she hadn't married.'

'I wonder if she'll take to wearing a veil and live in purdah. Arabs can have up to four wives, according to *The Qu'ran*.'

'If she has with her Moroccan what I had this summer with Jean-Paul, it'll be utter bliss! Sex is GREAT! How on *earth* I'm going to do without it for the next few months just doesn't bear *thinking* about!'

'You have boyfriends?' Aziz had asked.

'Oh, yes. There has usually been someone.'

'If you have me, then you must not have anyone else.'

She had smiled, oddly touched. None of the men she had known before had ever suggested they might be jealous if her interest strayed.

'Will you write to me?' had been the next question.

'You must give me your address.'

He had written it out for her, painstakingly, in capitals.

'Is good address,' he had reassured her.

The next question. 'Have you a photograph?'

She shook her head. It was a long time since anyone had taken a photograph of her. Moreover, she didn't photograph well.

'Will you send me one?'

'Why not?'

'You will remember?'

'Of course.'

'Are you sure I can't offer you a drink?'

'Quite sure, thank you, after all that mint tea. But perhaps I could have a bottle of mineral water for the journey tomorrow?'

'No problem. I give it to you when you go to bed.'

But when, half an hour later, she had finally gone to bed, they had both forgotten about the boring old mineral water. He had accompanied her up to the hotel reception lobby and handed her her room key. Then he had placed his hands on her shoulders and kissed her on both cheeks.

'Bonsoir.'

'Bonsoir.'

'I have been very serious with you. You will not tell anyone?'

'Trust me.'

'And you will write to me?'

'Yes.'

'Because I like you very much.'

It was a very intent, private moment, touched with a suppressed eroticism, like the gentle beating of wings. That was the real beginning. Later, she was to reflect with surprise, even a mild shock, that it had taken place in such a public setting.

WILMA MURRAY

A HOUSE ON CHRISTMAS HILL

'Martin, where are we going?'

'You'll see. It's not far now.'

'You said that ten minutes ago.' Kathy wrapped herself
more tightly in her sulk in the front seat of the mini and concentrated on willing up a blizzard over the monochrome
winter landscape.

They stopped at last on a farm track. With manic leaps
and a lot of silly smiling, Martin led her to a gate, opened it
and stepped aside with exaggerated courtesy to let her pass
through.

'It's just a field,' she said.

'But not just any field. It's our field. Well, the firm's field.
They've bought it to develop. What do you think?'

'What do you want me to say? It's a field.'

'But imagine it. We're going to build ten luxury houses
here. See those trees? The pines on the rise with the snow on
them? Doesn't it look just like a Christmas card? We're going
to call it Christmas Hill. That was my idea, actually.'

'Well, well. But it's not a bit like a Christmas card. There's
no coach and horses.'

'But do you like it?'

'Does it matter?'

'We could have a house up here some day. I have all the
plans in the car. Come on.'

'Hey! Hold on ... ' But he was already gone, head in,
backside out, rummaging in the back seat of the car.

He spread the plans out over the dashboard and steering
wheel, talking non-stop, punctuating his speech with an insistent prodding finger. Kathy focussed only on his upper lip
and let herself become slowly mesmerised by the sight of
his teeth appearing and disappearing in some busy comic pursuit of their own. When she tired of that, she pretended she
was a foreigner and had to struggle hard with his broad Scottish vowel sounds. None of it worked. She could still hear
what he was saying.

'You can see it all already, can't you?' she said, without

waiting for a gap in the flow of words.
'Of course I can.'
'Show me, then. Show me this house you'd like us to have.'
'This one. Look. The one on the corner at the top of the hill.'
'That's no good. I want to really see it. Now.'
'O.K. Get your scarf and gloves and come on.'
He ran to the top of the hill, his jeans white to the knees with powdery dry snow. She followed more slowly, hunched in her coat and determined to be thoroughly miserable.
With a stick, he outlined the plan of the house on the fresh snow, counting steps for measurement. Then he began to draw in the rooms, one by one, leaving gaps for doors.
'Stop!' he shouted at her as she threatened to wander into the plan. 'It's not finished.'
He piled so many words and images in front of her that she was forced at last to see the house. He leapt from room to room, describing and explaining, building walls out of his enthusiasm.
'It's done. You can come in now. But use the front door.'
'Georgian style, I presume,' she said. 'Two locks, a peep-hole and a chain on the inside. What are we afraid of, Martin?'
'It's a very secluded site. And we're rich.'
'My mini's going to look a bit out of place in the drive.'
'Oh, but we have a Range Rover now.'
She stood inside the space he had called the combo sitting room-dining room and looked around, assessing the decor.
'I don't like white walls. And there's no fireplace. I want a fireplace, with logs and real flames'
'And a washhouse and an outside loo?'
'Lavvy. We say lavvy.'
'Not any more we don't.'
'I see.' She wandered into the kitchen space. 'What do you see me doing in here?'
'Oh, rustling up a great dinner for the boss and his wife or a steak for me on a Saturday night.'
'Give me the stick a minute.' She began to draw in some squares round the kitchen walls.
'What are you doing?'
'That's the cooker. And the sink and the table.'
'No, no. It'll all be fitted. It's not going to be like the flat. Really, Kathy, you've no imagination.' He grabbed the stick back, rubbed her lines out with his foot and drew in his own

vision in the snow.

'O.K. Have it your way.' She turned her back on him and walked into the bedroom, smiling. 'Martin! There's a man looking in at me from that house over there.' She pointed down the empty field. 'He's always watching me. He's the bank manager with the big Volvo and the leather golf bag. His wife keeps asking me over for coffee to show off the antiques she buys at country sales. Are you going to speak to him, Martin?'

'I'll punch his face in. Or. We could have our bedroom in the back, of course.'

He followed her out into the back garden with this suggestion.

'Do we have a dog?' she asked.

'Yes.'

'Well, our dog's just shit on our next door neighbour's lawn. I'm hanging out the washing and she's giving me dirty looks. She's the retired schoolmistress, by the way. The one with the cats. Why don't you train the dog better, Martin?'

'That'll be your job. Anyway, you won't be hanging out the washing. You have a tumble drier. I told you. In the utility room.'

'O.K. So I'm pruning roses, then. We have lots of roses round the patio. Don't we, Martin? Well trained roses and a badly trained dog.'

'Kathy, stop this.'

'And are we letting our little Martin play with the American kids down the road? They're always in here, you know, asking for him and wolfing our cookies. But then you're never here, so you wouldn't know. But the parents are very liberated, so I hear. Whatever that means.'

'They probably hold fancy dress parties and have baths together.'

'You're getting the hang of this, Martin.'

'And you're showing yourself up.'

'Who to? Anyway, I don't like this house. It makes me unhappy. It makes me want to scream.'

'Don't you dare.'

'I will.' And she screamed three great ringing screams which carried across the field and hung locked in the cold air for what seemed like several minutes.

'For God's sake, Kathy.' He grabbed at her and she pulled away. 'Somebody might hear you.'

He grabbed at her again and they blundered around in an

undignified struggle, obliterating all trace of his carefully drawn plan. She struggled free and stood panting white breath.

'See? Nobody came. I don't want to live in a house where nobody comes when I scream. And you're no damned use. You're only worried about what the neighbours will think. Well, they can think what they like. I'm leaving you.'

She ran then, leaping through the powdered snow, straight down the field and slammed into the mini's driving seat.

'I can't stay with you, Martin,' she shouted up at him as he came down the field to the car. 'I don't like the house and I hate the neighbours.'

'It doesn't have to be like that,' he said, leaning in the window of the car.

'You're bloody right, it doesn't.' She moved over into the passenger seat. 'Come on. Get in, you silly sod.'

PAT GERBER

LONG WINTER SUNDAY

'Hey Ma! Come on, we're nearly at the top. Look!'

Muffled, numb, I plod uphill in deep snow. Wrapped in thick knitting, scarfed, gloved, socked and booted I feel nothing. The ski-goggles insulate my eyes, the hood my ears. Proof against all feeling I trudge upwards.

Pigeon breasts of snow feathered with fawn grasses quilt the hillside in soft hummocks. The father's black figure kicks bootsteps into the hill flank above me. The brothers scramble up and slide down with each footfall. Two of my sons.

'Ma look! This rock's completely covered in ice. Ouch! I'll exterminate you, creep!'

'Try it light of my life. I'm going to be at the top first — ha!'

Two sons. Always fighting, always vying with each other for success, attention, yet almost always good friends, separated by only a year, complete like twins.

Their voices sound bare, without resonance in the frozen air. There is no wind on this side of the mountain. Is Dumgoyne a mountain? Or merely a molehill?

There is the cairn, looking like a birthday cake, whiffs of snow streaking off the top like white ribbons. We'll feel the wind up there alright, high against the wide blue sky.

But I have three sons. The third should be snug in the carrying sack on my back. I lack his weight on my back. On previous Sunday walks his small body has kept me warm, and I him. The sack hangs empty on the kitchen hook.

The father and the two brothers are together above me. He is pointing out distant landmarks that they can see but I cannot, still pressed against the hillside. They seem oblivious, so close in their maleness, forgetful so soon.

Voices. My mother: 'The family — you are so lucky. A nice home, enough money, a good man who works hard to keep you all. You should be grateful.' A friend: 'The boys — you must pull yourself together. For their sakes.' My father: 'Your husband. Look to him. He bears the burden of responsibility for you all just now. You can't let him down.'

The hill steepens. One foot slips, then the other. I slide downwards grabbing with smothered, clawless fingers. All my efforts are wasted. I land in a heap at the bottom of the slope. Slow tears leak through the goggles and freeze on my cheeks. I have not cried, till now.

I look up. The three of them are busy. Making snowballs. They laugh as they begin to fling soft flurries down at me. Laughing. Suddenly I hate them, the smiling father, the frolicking, forgetful boys.

The father has smiled on other women. For the sake of my family I have chosen not to notice these leerings. And for myself.

The family. Ripped and rent apart now. These boys have no need of me. They live in a man's world of hard metal cars and fighting. The cars are matchbox size but will grow in status. The fights are part of school playground life, of street life too. In a few brief years they'll slough me off — the old woman — in favour of freedom, the struggle to make their mark on the world. Then younger women will take them. What is the point of organising my life round them? What is the point of climbing this stupid hill? Because it is there?

And the little one. The dependant, my baby. This time seven Sundays ago I was holding his warm hand. Later, at noon, they took away the plastic tent. At twelve minutes past he died. His live hand died in mine. I, who had first felt the flutter of his tiny feet within me, alone, privately, had been condemned to feel his last small breath alone. I alone bore my child company in his passing. For him, for myself and to protect the family from anguish, the father who couldn't bear it. Born when the green buds opened, he lived only a leaf's length of time and in December died. My mind tolls each dull fact one by one as it has done daily these past weeks, but today each intolerable blow strikes the very quick of bare nerves. I press my goggled face into the snow and scream with overfull lungs.

Every day for three months I had driven to the hospital to care for him. Every day on that journey through the darkening autumn days I had sung the twenty-third psalm over and over, as a prayer, a hope, a talisman — 'And tho' I walk through death's dark vale, yet wi-ill I fear none ill, for thou art with me, a-and thy rod, and sta-aff me comfort still' — if I reached the end of that verse before passing a certain ploughed field, everything would be alright. But it wasn't. Neither the prayer nor the talisman worked.

Now it is the very dead of winter. Men on the moon, they had said, yet this disease hasn't been researched. No cure — we'll try cortisone, it has worked on some American children, do you accept the risk? Then sign here. My small Scot was killed by my acceptance of his risk.

White ribbons and snowdrops from a shop on his small pale coffin. Had I wanted him to be cremated or buried? I could have whatever I wanted, they said. No, no I wanted *him*. For three nights I tussled alone with the choice between flames consuming or worms devouring the little hands, the perfect little toes, the chunky baby body, the blue eyes of my darling.

Fire I picked in the end, for its cleansing speed. But buried, not scattered, is the small box of grey ash, so that one day I may lie again beside him.

For me, now, God is dead. And I am condemned to life, because it is there.

'Are you coming up or not?' The father shouts from his ridge.

Another snowball hits me. Suddenly, anger flares. Why, why should that loved child have died? 'One of God's flowers, needed in Heaven, too good for this world' had mouthed the church-wives, platitudes boosting their beliefs. But he was needed here, here in my arms against my breast, sucking, warm and safe. I however had not been strong enough to save him, had failed him in his mortal struggle. And all these women aborting, and unloved starving waifs.

I strip off the steamed-up stupid goggles, pull back the deafening hood, rip off the gloves. I will climb this hill to the brim. More snowballs fall around me. I move around the base of this last slope, find a place where no foot has trodden the snow. Here my boots grip more surely, snow squeaking under my weight as I climb slowly at first.

I can smell the snow, green-white, in front of my face. I scuffle two handfuls into a ball and hurl it towards the summit.

'Hey look, Ma's going to make it! Stop bombing!'

'O.K. O.K. C'mon old Ma we'll give you a pull!'

My blood heats with effort, my breath gusts dragonlike steam-puffs. I lean a moment on iced rock. The last pitch looks perpendicular. The north face of the Eiger. I dare not look back now, or down. Too far to fall.

Other women have been here before me, I say to my-self. Other women have reached the summit, suffered and overcome. Three children out of Grandma's dozen sickened and died in childhood. I used to think that in those olden days the women must have expected to lose a proportion of their children, so it couldn't have been so bad. I do not think so now. Dark skeletal women draped in dusty African robes had stared out at me through the television screen over the stick-limbed bodies of their starving children. I had thought it must be almost normal for them, their babies dying daily. I do not think so now.

Pushing off again upwards, towards the skyline, I think that I am more fortunate than they. What have I done particularly to deserve my two remaining, rudely healthy sons?

Now the snow has been flayed away by the wind. Tussocks of frost-stiffened grass stick to juts of stone, and hidden under a ledge, green velvet moss cushions my raw and bleeding fingers. As I near the top edge of the summit, sunshine warms my shoulders.

'You two push, I'll pull.' The father's black gloved hand reaches down to me and four smaller hands shovel me over the last rock. For a minute I lie on my belly, gasping with effort expended. 'Well done', he says.

'Look Ma! I'm going even to the top of the cairn!'

Meanwhile his brother has scrambled up and stands there, triumphant against the blue sky. A fight follows. I switch my ears to tune in on the wind-song of two white swans flying low.

Standing now, I can feel the whip of freezing wind, but I do not care. I can see clearly all the wavy edges of my circular horizon. And I am in the middle of it. Eastward lies the blue-white snow covering the Campsies. Straight ahead runs the forest-dark valley of the Blane then murky fog blankets Glasgow, stuck with square pegs of concrete, laced with pylon wires. Beyond lurk the Gleniffer Braes. To the west, low hills dip to reveal a sliver of Loch Lomond and behind, a cyclorama of sharp white peaks against blue sky rolls to the muscular shoulder of the Ben, light-shirted, kilted in pines. The snowline is clearly defined halfway down my circle of hills. Below they are furred with woods, wrapped in warm bracken, patched and padded with fat green fields.

'I will lift mine eyes unto the hills from whence cometh my aid.' So small. So small and insignificant am I, invisible to anyone standing on any of these surrounding ranges, yet for a few brief years the centre of my childrens' strength.

'Look boys, that's where we live.' I begin to point out

landmarks, their father names distant mountains; 'The Cobbler, see? Ben An.' They are cold now, so we encircle them for warmth and share a chocolate bar.

We slither downhill towards the westering sun till the snow-line wanes. We ploughter thigh-high through tangled heather clumps to reach the bronze strip of bracken. The birchwood smells of damp green mosses as we follow an old track down to the waiting car. It steams up inside as we drive home.

'Can we have a fire?' The boys carry logs in from the shed and their father, my husband, makes scarlet and gold flames crackle cheerfully. Woodsmoke follows me from the imperfect chimney into the kitchen.

Standing by the warm grill I make toast and spread it with melting butter, brown sugar and drifts of cinnamon. Outside, beyond the window, the sun is sliding blue shadows across the garden, and I see the first snowdrop, green and white, gleaming above the black earth.

VALERIE GILLIES

INFERTILITY PATIENT

'I could never have enough children.' Katherine Mansfield

To lift another woman's child
is like carrying a bundle of barbed wire.
And one who will let himself be held
stirs every bereaved desire.

Between collarbone and breast
his hard head makes an impression:
a dent in a white quilt
someone's secretly been sleeping on.

My hands fall empty in my lap
when she lifts him away.
I can share, as I give him up,
only his backwards look with no wave.

She's the fertile one while I am not.
Inject a dye and see my tubes are drawn
blocked and scarred, death's first print I've got
in me: you month, rat's jaw, I see you yawn.

THE NET SINKER

White boat, do not leave me alone
at the edge of the ocean.

My tall yellowhaired helmsman
leant out, leant out
leant out over the water
and let fall the weighted cask.

He buried my loveletters to him
under seething waves, under seething waves
under waves where no-one could read them
or see my photograph alongside seatrout.

The sound of water at his boat's foot
where he knew, where he knew
where he knew the strait to be very deep
he dropped it and the sea accepted it.

The stone star's fall through the curving waves
words of mine, words of mine
written words of mine like net sinkers
fell to the depths of his mind.

Since then the rain's hissing or the sea's mumbling
my first singing, my first singing
hear my first singing and take your boat out
to where the waves kiss and kiss again.

In the south-east I walk out in the storm
let it drift, let it drift
let your heart drift over its diaphragm of sand
and turn still warm to me.

White boat, do not leave me alone.

THE OLD WOMAN'S REEL

She is at the small deep window
looking through and out:
the Aran islands, rock and seawater,
lie all about.
A face strong in poverty's hauteur
is hers, then and now.

Being a young woman in Flaherty's film
'Man of Aran',
she nearly drowned in the undertow
by the boat where she ran.
He kept on filming even though
he thought her dead on the rockrim.

A body plaited by water twine
they carried ashore:
partnered in the ocean's set dance
by two men or more.
The sea had had its chance
to peel her off by the shoreline.

Now in her great old age
toothless and tough,
the island music still delights her:
one dance is not enough.
The tunes of a people poor and cut off there
have a special power to engage.

Drawn upright, her stiff bones
already dancing,
she spins, not on one foot
but on her stick, tap-balancing.
While to one side like a pliant offshoot
a little girl mimics her, unbeknown.

ROBBIE KYDD

TOOLS, SKILLS, AND FEELING SMALL

Andy tries to copy the figure 7 from the blackboard on to the clean new page of his jotter. His pencil wobbles and the 7 looks like a worm. He tries again and it looks like another worm. He tries a third time and it looks like a worm that someone has tried to bite in half.

Andy looks to his left. Fiona, at the next oak-and-iron desk, has drawn a whole line of beautiful 7s, almost as good as Miss Hood's on the blackboard. Miss Hood isn't looking, she is bending over someone at the front of the class, so Andy finishes his line of 7s in a rush. They look like a fence that is falling down.

He glances to his left again. Fiona is sitting up 'properly', holding her pencil 'properly' in her plump fingers. She is half-way through her second line of 7s, all of them perfect.

He looks to his right. Geordie, who shares his desk, is working hard. His short legs are twisted together and his head is almost on the desk and his tongue is sticking out. He has drawn two careful 7s, almost as perfect as Fiona's. He untwists his legs, twists them again the other way round, licks his pencil, and starts on his third 7. Geordie is slow but sure, Miss Hood says, but she'll be cross if she sees him licking his pencil.

My big brother, Andy thinks, writes his figures *very very* fast and they come out like Miss Hood's, so he does his second line *very very* fast. They come out like a line of telephone poles getting bigger and bigger and more and more uneven. He looks up and Miss Hood is arriving at his desk, smelling of peppermints and leather shoes. He black gown is dusty with chalk. She has a 'lady' smell too, so Andy tries to hold his breath.

'You must be more careful,' she says, bending down from her great height and putting his fingers round his pencil 'properly'. She guides his hand to make the first 7 of his third row. It is, of course, nearly perfect.

'Now try that yourself,' says Miss Hood. Andy tries. He breaks the point of his pencil. He is too frightened to look up.

'Careless boy!' he hears Miss Hood saying crossly. She isn't really angry though. She reaches into the deep flying pocket of her gown for a pencil sharpener, sharpens Andy's pencil, and moves away to someone else after pleased glances at Fiona and Geordie. Andy can't sharpen a pencil. His big brother can.

Andy needs to go to the bathroom, but he doesn't want to ask Miss Hood if he may leave the room. She'll still be cross with him, after the broken pencil. He presses his legs together and hopes for the best. He tries another 7 and it looks like a squashed worm. The next he tries is better but much too big. The next is almost perfect, but even bigger.

Fiona, Andy can see, has finished a whole neat page of proper 7s, all the same height. Her finger-nails are round at the top, a much nicer shape than his blunt ones. They are spotless underneath too, while his are black. His big sister says, 'Your nails are going to a funeral'. Andy wishes he could hide them. The pleats in Fiona's kilt are perfect.

The playtime bell, it must ring soon. Andy breaks his pencil again, but pretends to go on writing. Fiona turns to him, half closes her eyes, and puts out the tip of her pink tongue. She looks at the mistakes in his jotter, opens her eyes wide, and makes an O of her mouth. She has noticed! Why does he have to sit in the row next the girls? None of the boys want to sit there. It was Miss Hood who made him. Andy wishes with all his heart that he was right at the other end of his room. Not that he wants to leave Geordie, who is his friend.

His friend is sighing and straightening out his legs. He is wearing a khaki jersey several sizes too large for him which would fit a very wee soldier, ragged tweed shorts, odd stockings with holes in them right down round his ankles, and gym-shoes without laces, but he doesn't care. He doesn't care a bit. His legs are short and thick and dirty and sunburned. Andy glances down at his own scrawny, warty, clean, pale knees sticking out between his clean flannel shorts and his clean grey carefully darned stockings. His tackety boots are shiny. Dad cleans them, laughing about Mother getting the vote. Grown-ups have boring secrets. Andy can't run as fast as Geordie, or kick a ball so cleverly and fiercely, and he never gets sunburned. He wants to go to the bathroom — it's called the 'lavvy' at school.

The playtime bell goes at last, but Miss Hood is slow about letting the class out. Andy thinks he is going to wet his pants, but she goes on fussing about passing forward and counting the pencils. Pencils are precious, because of the War. So are jotters. Then everybody has to sit up straight enough to please Miss Hood, which is very straight indeed. After she is satisfied that everyone is like a poker, she gives the magic signal and Andy marches out with the others.

He runs across the playground, weaving and dodging to avoid the crowds of other boys, also weaving and dodging. He reaches the outside 'lavvy', but stops dead when he meets the smell of fresh pee and disinfectant and old pee. It seems to be pouring out of the door. To make things worse, there is a lot of shouting and giggling going on inside. The big boys from Standard Five, they will be showing each other how high they can pee. They were doing it yesterday. They are always doing it. Sometimes the Jannie shouts at them, but as soon as he's gone they start again.

Andy has *got* to pee, so he rushes through the big urinal where the game is going on, opens the door of the first w.c. and manages to lock himself in. Sometimes the locks are too stiff for him. Sometimes the locks have been torn off. A big boy must be peeing really high for a fine spray is coming over the partition, but Andy is in too much of a hurry to notice. He unbuttons his trousers and looks into the lavvy. The water is brown and it has a lot of other boys' froth on it. He can't pee. Oh dear. He pulls the chain and the noise of rushing water makes his thingie sore. The water stops rushing and his pee comes spouting out and splashes over the seat and the floor and everything. He manages to point his pee at the water in the lavvy, where it makes a few bubbles, which quickly disappear. Why doesn't his pee make a froth? Andy is sure that Geordie's pee makes a froth.

Andy buttons up his trousers, opens the door of the w.c. and makes a dash for the playground. Free at last! He runs round and round, giving a small yell every so often. I can run. I can run. I can run. He changes to a gallop, slapping his behind. I'm a cowboy on his horse. Giddy-up! Giddy-up! Giddy-up! Andy is not allowed to go to the pictures but Geordie has told him all about the cowboys there, kindly explaining the still photos in their glass cases outside the Grand Cinema.

Andy gallops in and out of the big boys' football game, but they take no notice of him. He gallops right to the front of the playground. He has to be careful here, for just across the road is the Catholic school. The playground over there is rough gravel and some of the big Catholic boys can throw stones right across. Catholics are even rougher than the rough boys here. 'I can fight papes,' says Geordie, 'they're jist a lotta tattie-howkers.' Mother would be very very angry if she caught Andy fighting. She doesn't even let him shove his big brother when his big brother has just shoved him.

Andy gallops away to where Geordie is kicking a very old tennis ball furiously against the school wall, all by himself. Geordie is too small for the big boys' game, and nobody his own age wants to play with him because he is too good. Geordie takes no notice of Andy so he gallops on, but he has to stop suddenly when he sees Fiona in the girls' playground on the other side of the spiked iron railings. She is stotting a ball cleverly and singing a stotting song, watched by a group of girls. They see him looking and turn to each other and smile as if they knew a secret. Fiona sees him too, half-closes her eyes, thrusts out her pink lower lip and turns her stotting into a kind of dare. Andy knows it's a dare because Fiona used to be his friend before they started school. They played together every day. It's a silly dare, because he couldn't stot a ball in the boys' playground even if he had one. Balls are for kicking. He wants to shout 'fatty!' at her. Instead, he runs away and finds a quiet spot round the corner of the building.

There is a haipny in the right hand pocket of his trousers. Where did it come from? Maybe Mother put it there. Maybe it was left over from his Saturday penny and he forgot about it. It is his to spend, anyway. He decides to buy a poke of toffee at Beardie Jean's on his way back to school after dinner. Mother doesn't like him going there because Beardie Jean smears her toffee-tins with beef dripping and she never washes her hands and she puts vinegar in her toffee. Mother can smell vinegar a mile off, whether from forbidden chips or forbidden toffee. The toffee is nice, though, sweet and sharp and greasy, in big splinters like brown glass, and you can chew it for a long time.

Beardie Jean's pokes are made of newspaper and Andy isn't too happy about them. 'Where has that newspaper been?' asks Mother. She tears newspapers into squares and threads a piece of string through them with a big needle and hangs them up beside the lavvy. Fiona has toilet paper in her house because her father works in a bank. Beardie Jean's toffee is really really nice, all the same.

Playtime seems to have lasted for ever, so it must be nearly over. Andy remembers that it will be reading and writing next, so he runs to the boys' door to be first in the line when the bell goes. The Jannie comes out in his shiny-peaked hat and clangs the big brass bell and Andy has to fight for his place at the head of the line. Geordie pushes and elbows him and he has to take second place. He would cry if it wasn't Geordie. Mr Calder, who teaches the Qualifying, appears at the top of the steps and the boys go silent and still, for he was wounded in the War, has a nasty tongue, and belts very hard when he does belt. He marches the boys in, class by class.

Andy runs to his desk, sits down and opens his reading-book happily. He has reached the very last story in the book although it is only two weeks since school started. Mother likes that. She was hearing his reading homework last night and he showed her that he could read the first page of the last story. She hugged him, but he wasn't sure that he liked being babied.

Dad, who had put down his paper, saw the hug and said, 'Don't get too brainy, will you. We don't go in for geniuses in our family.' Then he laughed, even though he hadn't said anything funny.

His big brother said, 'Swot! Swot! Swot!'

His big sister said, 'You're soft on Fiona Phimister.'

'No, I'm not,' protested Andy. 'I bet she can't read.' 'She can so!' 'She's got a tidemark round her neck.' 'No, she hasn't!' 'See! You're soft on her.'

Miss Hood tells everyone to open their books and find 'the place'. Andy finds the right page, puts his finger on the 'place' and turns the pages over his finger until he reaches the last story, but he can't start reading it until he has looked at Fiona's neck. She is sitting up properly with her finger at the 'place' and her neck does *not* have a tidemark. He can see it all because she has an 'Eton Crop' which is very short. It is a round smooth clean neck, as plump as the rest of Fiona, and the more he looks at it the funnier he feels, so he turns away.

Andy sits up just as properly as he can and starts to read the last story. At his side Geordie is lounging easily, with only an eye on 'the place'. Miss Hood will tell him to sit up in a minute, but Geordie doesn't care. Every time Andy has to turn a page he looks up at Miss Hood first, to make sure she isn't looking, but the story is so interesting that he forgets to keep his finger on 'the place'.

Miss Hood goes on hearing the reading, beginning with the worst readers at the front of the class. She will end up at the back, where Andy sits. Sometimes she starts at the back, but never in the middle. The worst readers have to read one sentence, the middle ones two sentences, and the best three sentences. This is the second year the class have had Miss Hood and Andy feels safe enough to lose himself in the story, which is a long one about King Arthur and his Knights. He is so lost that he doesn't notice when Geordie stands up to read his two sentences. As Geordie sits down he gives Andy a dig with his elbow at the exact moment that Miss Hood says 'Wake up!' sharply.

Andy stands up, but he has, of course, lost 'the place'. He looks at Fiona's book, but she immediately shuts it on her finger, just to stop him from seeing. She isn't his friend any more. Geordie pushes his book across the desk, his finger tapping the place, like the good friend he is. Andy reads, but not very well. He is much better at reading 'to himself' or to Mother. Miss Hood says, 'Speak up!' and he stumbles and has to start again. He reads two sentences and Miss Hood says 'That will do.' He isn't a good reader any more, he's only a middle reader.

'Now, Fiona,' Miss Hood says and Fiona stands up, holds her book in her two hands 'properly' and reads her three sentences in her clear, 'nice', almost English, voice. She sits down, arranges her kilt neatly over her fat knees, and puts her finger at 'the place'. Andy knows what she's doing, but can't bear to look or listen.

Everyone else in the class has their finger at the 'place'. Miss Hood has a strap and she uses it too. She will have her eye on Andy because he lost the place and did not read as well as she knows he can.

Fiona is sitting up with a serious face and seems to be paying attention to Miss Hood and the reading that is still going on. Quietly, she lifts her foot and kicks the girl in front of her, right on her behind. The girl is the tallest and slimmest and prettiest in the class, with fair hair in long pig-tails and big blue eyes. Her name is Pamela and she is Miss Hood's pet, always going messages and helping with the register. She has rows of medals for Highland dancing and Geordie says she is stuck-up but Andy secretly worships her. He wouldn't dare to speak to her. Fiona hates her and tells everybody. She kicks Pamela again. Pamela jumps and looks as if she is going to hold up her hand and clype, but she doesn't. Miss Hood will catch Fiona one day, but she won't get the strap. Girls are lucky, not getting the strap.

Andy forgets the girls and the strap and goes back to the last story, remembering this time to put his finger firmly on a pretend place. When he has finished the story he tries to read the tiny print at the bottom of the page which says 'Printed in Great Britain by . . . ' but it is too difficult. He looks back at the other stories and pictures, but he knows them all too well to read them again. Geordie is dribbling with a pretend ball under the desk. Fiona is gazing at Miss Hood and then at Pamela and then back at Miss Hood. Andy drifts off into a day-dream about King Arthur.

He is roused by the end of the reading lesson. Miss Hood has gone back to her desk and is looking round the class. Her long face seems quite kind. She is going to say, 'Take out your writing jotters'. She says it.

Andy is good at writing — not as good as Fiona, but better than almost anyone else. Letters have nice friendly shapes, unlike figures, which are used for sums. Horrible sums. He sits 'properly' and puts his left hand 'properly' half on the desk and half on the jotter. He grips his pencil properly and does exactly what Miss Hood says. He writes a lovely round capital A. A for Andy. A for Apple. He writes a second one and then a third. He has written a whole line, all the same size, just as Miss Hood says he should. He could write capital As for ever. He likes Miss Hood and everybody in the whole world.

Andy knows that there has been trouble over that capital A but he manages to forget about it. Miss Hood prefers the capital A that looks like a witch's hat with a squiggle across it, but the Rector came in one day to change things. He said that in future capital As would be the round kind, like a small a. It was something to do with the new world after the War. Miss Hood had made a face behind the Rector's back. Everyone had to learn to write the round A, but Miss Hood now turns a blind eye to witch's hats and everyone but Andy has gone back to them. They are in the copy-books and on the wall-charts.

Miss Hood says things like, 'That's a baby kind of capital A'. So does his big brother. His big sister says, 'I bet Fiona Phimister can't write,' but Andy takes no notice. Mother says, 'The Rector must know what's right.' Dad, who is a teacher himself, says, 'Miss Hood should be boss in her own class-room.' Andy just carries on writing it, for it is his own very special A now, his very own. Miss Hood can't stop him, for the Rector is on his side.

He and Fiona finish their pages of As so quickly that Miss
Hood says, 'Go on to the capital Bs'. Fiona's first line of Bs is
a work of art. She goes to her second calmly. Andy also starts
on his Bs, which are nice but not so nice as As. Geordie is
nearly half-way through his page of As and his witch's hats
manage to look nearly as fierce as he is. It's nice to have a
fierce friend, Andy thinks, getting fed up with writing single
letters. He seems to have been doing it for months and months.
Miss Hood is far away and not looking so he turns to the
back page of his jotter and writes 'Andy'. He does it again
and again until he has done it ten times. He looks up, but
Miss Hood is not looking. Fiona and Geordie are busy and
have not noticed what he is up to. He writes 'Andy is a good
boy' right across the page from one side to the other.

The other children are beginning to be restless, wanting
their dinners. They are sniffling and coughing and shifting
about in their seats — but quietly, of course, because of the
strap. Andy isn't noticing that he's hungry and writes his sentence again and again until the page is full. He does not hear
Miss Hood approaching.

'What are you doing, Andy Robb?' she demands, tall and
frightening in her black gown, 'that jotter is for *work*, not
scribbling. Haven't I told you how precious paper is? Men
have *died* so that you can have jotters. Go and stand in the
floor.'

Andy goes and stands by her desk. It is taller than him
and the strap's inside it, coiled like a snake. He puts his hand
in his pocket and holds his haipny tight. Miss Hood gave
Geordie the strap for standing on his desk and shouting
'Come on, the Rangers!' just as she was coming into the
room. Now she is fussing about passing forward and counting
the pencils. Fiona, as she goes past, looks at Andy with wide-
open eyes. Is she glad or sorry? He can't tell. Once she held
his head when he hurt it falling off a forbidden wall and
daren't run home to Mother. Her hands were softer than
Mother's. Now he can hear the children yelling as they leave
the playground on their way home to dinner. Miss Hood is
taking her time about coming back. Maybe she's gone to tell
the Rector about him.

Miss Hood returns at last, goes straight to her desk, opens
it and takes out the strap.

'Hold out your hand,' she says. He lets go of his haipny
and holds out his hand.

'Not like that! Right out!' He stretches his hand right out.

The strap is thick, like the sole of a boot, and has a long slit at the end. It comes down out of the sky on to his fingers and a terrible soreness fills the world, the whole universe, and then rushes to his fingers. They've suddenly become ten times as big as they ought to be. There is an enormous slamming noise and Andy nearly faints, but it is only Miss Hood dropping the lid of her desk.

'You can tell your mother *why* I gave you the strap,' she says, shooing him out.

His arm will never be able to carry the weight of the soreness in his hand, his enormous hand. His arm feels as if it might come out of its socket. His eyes are ready to water. Mother wouldn't like him to hate Miss Hood, so he doesn't. Not now, anyway.

Geordie and one or two of the other boys have waited for him at the school gate. Fiona is nowhere to be seen — she must have run home.

'Wis it sair?' the boys ask. He daren't cry now.

'Aye, it wis sair,' he answers. Mother wouldn't like to hear him talk like that, but he must. He is now one of the bad boys who have had the strap, and that is the way they all talk. He shows the boys his fingers and is surprised they are not swollen, only red. Geordie puts a friendly arm around his shoulders.

'When she gied me the strap,' he says, 'she missed ma hand an hut me on the wrist an it swellt richt up. Did she hut yer thumb?'

'Naw, she didnae.'

'Ye're aa richt, then. When she huts that bane in yer thumb, then ye'll greet. Ye should try blawin on yer fingers.'

Just talking about them makes Andy's fingers seem smaller, but they are just as sore in a different way. They feel like bare bones. He blows into them as Geordie has suggested, but it doesn't help much. The other boys have drifted away.

Geordie turns and runs and Andy runs after him, the pain almost forgotten. Geordie starts to hop and skip and Andy copies him, the pain just a nuisance. At the corner of the road to the council houses, where Geordie lives, some big Catholic boys are waiting, doing nothing in particular. Catholics often don't eat dinner, explained Fiona's mother once, in a kind voice. Geordie runs past the loiterers, towards home, as fast as he can. Andy runs as fast as *he* can, up the main road to his corner, by the sweetie-shop. He turns and looks back, but the Catholic boys have vanished. His fingers still hurt, he finds, now that he has nothing else to think about. They are hot, like four chips straight out of the pan. He tries sucking them, but they don't cool down.

The window of the sweetie-shop attracts Andy's attention, and he forgets his fingers. There are aniseed balls and black-strippit balls and sugar-elly straps and sherbet bags, all a haipny each. He looks them over and decides he prefers Beardie Jean's toffee — you get more of it. He'll go to school the back way after dinner and buy some. Bars of chocolate are tuppence so he tries not to think about them.

He has a last look at the shop window. At the back, beside the pencils and rubbers and envelopes, there is a little note-book. He can read NOTE BOOK in smudgy print on the front cover. What's more, it has '½d' written on it in pencil in the top corner. Andy gets excited, for he realises that it could be his. He could have his own writing-book, his very own. Where would he find a pencil? Forgetting the pencil, he fondles his haipny, and thinks about Beardie Jean's sticky-sweet toffee. Then his fingers start to sting again and he has to suck them. He remembers that Mother will be wondering where he is. He should have been home by now. He runs home as fast as he can.

Mother is fussing, as usual.

'Where have you been?' she asks. 'You're late.' Not answering is the best plan. 'Hurry up and wash your hands.'

Dinner is mince and tatties, his favourite. They are almost cold, so he can eat them very quickly, thinking about the note-book. He feels for his haipny — it is safe.

'Why are you smelling so horrid?' asks Mother, 'You haven't wet yourself, have you?' Not answering is still the best plan.

His big brother sniffs loudly. His big sister giggles.

'He sits next Geordie MacMillan and he plays with him all the time,' she says, 'no wonder he smells.' She giggles again. Clype!

'Go upstairs and change your underpants,' says Mother. Andy goes upstairs, sits on his bed for a while and comes back down.

'That feels better, doesn't it?' says Mother. Not answering again works.

'You'll be late for school!' she says, as she always does. Andy rushes off, one hand in the pocket where the haipny is.

He runs fast till he reaches the end of the narrow lane that leads to Beardie Jean's. He stops. He must decide. It is

either down that way and buy a poke of toffee or straight on
and buy the note-book. His fingers are still telling him that he
was belted. He hops up and down. He 'runs on the spot' with
his knees right up. He says, 'Eanie, meanie, mynie, mo' and
the note-book wins, much to his relief. He would have to
give Geordie a bit of the toffee and Fiona would see it and de-
mand some and it would be finished by the end of afternoon
play-time. The note-book he can keep for ever. He can take it
to bed with him.

The lady in the shop is neat and clean, not like Beardie
Jean at all. She takes Andy's haipny and gives him the note-
book without changing her expression or saying anything,
but Andy doesn't care. The note-book is his. It has a pale
green paper cover and the lines on the pages inside are really
close together. He will write like his big brother, really small,
and as neatly as Fiona. Where can he get a pencil? The note-
book smells delicious — like nothing else on earth. It is properly stitched together, too, like a school jotter. Andy dawdles
along, opening it and sniffing it and stroking the smooth
pages.

He reaches school just in time to be last in the line and
for once he doesn't care. He hides his note-book under his
jersey, which is not a very safe place, so he grips it through
his jersey as firmly as he can. When he reaches his desk, he
decides to put it in his school-bag. Geordie sees him putting it
away.

'Ye bocht that?' he asks.

'Yes,' Andy has to answer.

'Ye're stupit! Ye could a had a haipny's worth at Beardie
Jean's,' says Geordie, but he is not really cross. He is still a
friend.

Miss Hood calls for silence, and gets it. She calls for
Pamela to help her hand out the tins of crayons and the
drawing books. She reminds the children that they must not
waste the crayons, which are even more precious than pencils,
or the six-inch-square coloured paper drawing books.

Andy looks at the drawing he did last week. It is on a
green page and it is supposed to be a flower. It doesn't look
like a flower at all, never mind the flower that Miss Hood
told them to draw. It looks like a baby's drawing, all scrawly.

Fiona's flower is really wonderful and makes the green
page look greener. He'll never draw like Fiona.

Geordie's flower looks like a red-white-and-blue Rangers
rosette and his green page looks like a football pitch after a

muddy game.

Miss Hood announces that today's page is the brown one and that they are to draw an apple. She puts an apple on the top of her desk where they can all see it. It is a red Canadian apple, just like the ones Mother buys, with a yellow streak and a long stalk.

Andy opens the dusty little crayon box. None of the crayons are more than an inch long and they have all lost their paper covering, so he knows he will get his hands dirty. Mother won't like that. He chooses a scrap of red crayon and, without thinking, writes a huge round capital A, right in the middle of the page. He is terrified when he sees what he has done, for it isn't an apple. It has *two* little stalks, little *red* stalks, at one side instead of just one at the top. He puts his hand on it to hide it but realises that his hand will smudge the crayon, so he lifts it a little, and looks at Fiona.

Fiona has outlined a perfect red heart and, as Andy watches, writes ALP right across it. ALP means 'Andy Loves Pamela'. Girls are always writing stupid things like that. Geordie wouldn't ever write that.

Fiona smiles as if she knows a secret. She looks up at Miss Hood and Pamela, who are doing the register. She 'shades in' her heart, covering up the ALP, then adds a neat black stalk at the top. Then she fattens it until it becomes an apple. Pamela returns to her seat, looks at Fiona's book, and sniffs. Fiona looks at Miss Hood with a sweet expression and returns to her drawing. She picks up a yellow crayon and puts in the yellow streak. With the tip of her pinkie she carefully smudges the yellow until it looks exactly like the streak on the apple. She licks the crayon off her pinkie, sits up properly and gazes at Miss Hood. Then she kicks Pamela. Pamela turns round with a swing of her pig-tails and makes a horrible face.

'Fiona! Behave!' says Miss Hood. Andy suddenly remembers his note-book and forgets everything else for a while.

Geordie's head is down, as usual, and his tongue is out. His apple is a good shape, but it is smudged round the edges. It has a big black stalk which looks like the smoke coming out of a factory chimney. Geordie sighs. He smells of vinegar.

Andy lifts his hand off the brown page. He fattens up his apple just as Fiona has done, covering the two little stalks at the side. He shades it all in and puts in the yellow streak. Daintily, copying Fiona, he smudges the yellow with the tip of his pinkie. He licks his pinkie clean, but wishes he hadn't, for the crayon tastes dusty and nasty. Miss Hood comes round just as he is finishing off his apple with a dark green stalk.

'Would you like to write "apple" underneath?' she asks.

Andy is not happy about this, the others might think he was Miss Hood's pet, but the thought of the big capital A is too tempting. He picks up an orange crayon and writes a lovely A. He follows with two fat ps, a very very straight l, and a cheeky e. When he lifts his head he sees that the word is wobbly, because he had no line to guide him. He looks round fearfully. Miss Hood is coming. She looks at his brown page. It is spoilt.

'Go out to the floor and hold it up so that everyone can see it,' she says. Andy can't tell how angry she is. His fingers are still sore, but she might belt him on the other hand. He goes out to the floor, not daring to look at Fiona or Geordie or anyone else.

'Children,' Miss Hood says, 'look at Andy's drawing. It is by far the best today. He was the only one who saw that the stalk is green.'

Andy stands there, unable to think until he remembers his note-book, safe in his school-bag. He will write in it after school if he can find a pencil, or borrow one from his big brother. He won't tell him about the note-book, which he will hide under the mattress.

Miss Hood sends Andy back to his seat. Fiona is looking straight at him with a sweet smile on her face. Andy knows that it is not a nice smile at all.

'Copy-cat!' whispers Fiona. Andy sits down.

'That's guid!' says Geordie, looking at Andy's apple and dribbling his pretend ball under the desk.

At play-time Andy puts his note-book under his jersey and gets a good grip of it from the outside. He runs round and round the playground. As he passes the girls' railings Fiona sticks her head through and shouts 'Andy Robb is no good, chop him up for firewood!' She shouts it again and again and half-a-dozen other girls join in, so Andy runs to the front of the playground. There are no children in the Catholic school playground, so it is safe for him to walk up and down, fondling his note-book.

After play-time Miss Hood reads a story. It isn't a real story. Miss Hood reads it in a sad and trembly voice. It is about the soldiers who died for us and is even sadder than the Sunday School stories about Jesus dying for us. Andy is not

good at listening to these kind of stories. He isn't sure if the
soldiers and Jesus are the same and has a picture in his head
of a man in armour dying on a cross. He prefers King Arthur
or Robert the Bruce. The picture of the man on the cross
goes away and Andy goes on thinking about his note-book
and where to get a pencil and what secrets he will write about.

Geordie nudges him under the desk and he wakes up and
looks down. Geordie is offering him half a cold chip from the
pocket in his khaki jersey. Andy takes it. It smells nice and
vinegary. He manages to squeeze it round his mouth with his
tongue and then swallow it without chewing. If Miss Hood
saw him chewing during her sad story it would be the strap
again, and Mother would be told. Mother would then tell
Dad, and Dad would laugh at him again, and he couldn't bear
that. Geordie is watching Miss Hood and chewing openly. He
will be caught one day but he doesn't care.

The story ends and it's home time and Andy straps up his
school-bag and swings it on to his back. His note-book is still
under his jersey and he holds it tight. Once out of the playground he tries to run after Geordie, but Geordie is dribbling
his tennis ball faster than Andy can run, weaving in and out
of the gutter and round the people in the street.

Andy gives up the chase and thinks about his note-book.
He is wandering along, half in a dream and half keeping an
eye open for big Catholic boys, when Fiona overtakes him,
running. Her school-bag is bouncing on her back. He can run
faster than Fiona, for she's fat and he's skinny, so he starts to
run after her. He starts to catch up with her and she stops. He
has to stop, too.

They played together nearly every day before they went
to school, and they still do in the holidays, but now he's not
sure if he really wants to catch up with her. After all, he
knows he can run faster than her. Fiona starts to run again,
her fat legs moving fast. Andy runs too. She stops. He stops.
She runs again and doesn't stop until she reaches her house
and disappears through the gate in their privet hedge. He
slows to a walk. That silly girl hasn't made him forget his
note-book, for he is still holding it tight.

As he passes Fiona's gate she comes out. He stops. She
comes close up to him. She smells as she always does, clean.
Really clean. She could be his friend if she wasn't a girl. Why
does she have to be a girl? In the summer holidays her mother
lets her wear khaki shorts to play in the garden and with her
Eton Crop she looks like Billy Bunter. But she's so fat you

can see she hasn't got a thingie inside her shorts. Maybe he'll be able to play with her in the Christmas holidays — in her garden, not in the street.

'What have you got under your jersey?' she asks. She has noticed. She always notices.

'I'm not telling.'

'Is it a secret?' With Fiona it's no use pretending.

'Yes.'

'I won't tell. Cross my heart.' Andy is forced to tell.

'It's just a wee note-book.' He shows it to her.

'Oo! It's nice! Have you got a pencil for it?'

'No.'

'I'll get you one.' She runs into her house and comes out in a minute with an inch-long stub, properly sharpened. Andy takes it, not looking at Fiona. He tries to say, 'I'll give you a shottie of my note-book,' but half-way through he has to run away. If he gave her a shottie it wouldn't be his *very very* own any more.

Running away, he tries to tell himself that he is really running away from Fiona's mother, who is always coming out and asking him 'Where did you get that red curly hair? And those freckles?' He hates that, but it's even worse when she asks to feel his muscles, for he has no muscles, compared to Geordie.

'Copy-cat! Copy-cat!' Fiona is shouting after him.

When he reaches home Mother asks, 'Well, what happened in school today?' He can't think of anything to say, so he doesn't answer. He drops his school-bag in the hall and runs up to the bedroom he shares with his big brother. He hides his note-book and pencil under the mattress on his side of the double bed. I will be writing in it soon, he thinks, very soon.

He didn't go to the lavvy at school, so he's bursting. He rushes to the bathroom and pees properly, without splashing, but he forgets to wash his hands.

'Do you want a rock-bun?' calls Mother from downstairs.

'Yes!' he shouts, rushing down headlong.

'Have you washed your hands?'

'Yes, Mother,' he says, and has to stop where he is, just inside the kitchen door. He puts his hands behind his back. They are dirty from the crayons and half-a-dozen other things, never mind the bathroom.

'Here's your rock-bun.' He daren't take it.

'Show me your hands!' Mother is like Fiona, she *always*

notices. He shows her his hands.

'Who's been teaching you to tell lies? If it's that Geordie MacMillan, I'll go and see the Rector.' Saying nothing is the best plan. 'No bun! Go up to your room!'

Andy climbs the first few steps slowly, swallowing the spit that the rock-bun has made in his mouth. Then he remembers his note-book and runs up the rest. He shuts the door of the bedroom, takes out the note-book and pencil from under the mattress, and lies on the floor. He has half-an-hour until his big brother comes home and he's going to write for the whole time.

To start with, he writes very very small, but that is tiring and the pencil gets blunt too, so he decides that his letters will be two lines high. Then that gets tiring so his letters get three lines high. What he writes is a secret. He has trouble spelling Fiona's secret name, which is Greek. Only he and Fiona know about it. He has a secret name too, but it's easy to spell. Andy is lost in his secret world.

His big brother bursts into the room and, quick as lightening, grabs his note-book. He doesn't bother to read it, just flips roughly through the pages and throws it into the air.

'That's a waste of a good note-book,' he shouts, 'scribbling on it like a baby. You should learn to write properly.'

Andy snatches it back and crawls under the bed. His big brother reaches to pull him out, but he screams in the hope that Mother will hear. She doesn't seem to hear but she shouts 'Rock-buns!' which takes his big brother away much quicker.

Andy sees a gap under the skirting-board. It's a good hidey-hole so he slides his note-book into it. Then he lies under the bed and cries for quite a while for he hasn't got a nice new note-book any more, only a scribbled-on one. The secrets don't seem like secrets any more now that he has written them down. They're just scribbles, and for scribbles you get the strap. *And* deserve it, according to Dad, who would laugh, even though he was really serious. Mother would frown and ask if he had clean underpants.

Andy remembers his Saturday penny and cheers up. He could spend a haipny of it on another note-book and write proper stories in it and not secrets. With the other haipny he could buy a rubber to rub out mistakes. On Sunday he could spend half of his Sunday School penny at Beardie Jean's and put the other haipny in the plate. No one would notice, and there's no strap at Sunday School.

Andy sees the pencil Fiona gave him lying where he

dropped it. He comes out from under the bed and picks it up. It is blunt. He hides it under the mattress. He *must* learn to sharpen a pencil, he thinks, he really must.

ROBBIE KYDD

CAUGHT IN THE RYE

I was sure I was going mad . . . Otherwise, why was I standing
there on the verge of the by-pass, with the rain soaking my
tee-shirt and jeans and filling up my 'training' shoes, and my
mind inter-galactically empty, except for senseless phrases
orbitting round and round? My father's wrath broke upon me
. . . teacher of guidance . . . my father's wrath . . . guidance . . .

Cars and lorries were rushing past with headlights glaring,
throwing up fountains of spray which wet me even more. If
you were Holden Caulfield, I said to myself, you'd have a few
dollars to call a taxi and check in at a hotel and get drunk.
But you're not Holden, and it's Friday, and all the small
change you've got is 3½p from last Saturday's pocket money.
So you can't even afford a bus home, if that's where you
want to go . . .

The phrases went on orbitting relentlessly . . . I forced
myself to think about them, in case there was some sense in
them which would give me a lifeline back to sanity. Okay,
my father and I really had had a quarrel just before I left. It
was to do with being more regular about church on Sundays
and settling down to swot for more Highers than I want to
bother with. He also had a side-swipe or two at my Scottish Nationalist and Thatcherite friends, who exist almost
entirely in his imagination. I'm sure the pressure he was
exerting wasn't so much to do with my welfare as with his
own positions as Elder of the Kirk and (not, thank god, in
my school) Principal Teacher of Guidance. There it was again,
the senselessness . . . How could he teach 'guidance' to
children? He could maybe teach guidance *of* children to
other teachers, but *to* children, I can't see it. Yet if sane
people have decided on that title, I must be insane not to
understand it . . . Perhaps I've inherited some tendency,
some taint, from my father . . . He did seem mad when his
wrath broke upon me . . . Taint? Tendency?

A heavy lump of spray thrown up by a thundering lorry
hit me, cold, in the crutch and the animal in me demanded

that I find shelter before it shrivelled away altogether. I
hunched my shoulders and turned away from the insistent
wind and the threatening headlights on the nearer carriageway, the phrases echoing yet again in the black hole that was
my brain . . . wrath broke . . . teacher . . . wrath . . .
    I'm writing this in a real black hole with a contraband
ballpoint in a contraband jotter. Normally I churn out vast
quantities of fantasy (phantasy?) stuff — science fiction,
horror film scripts, spy stories and sic-like rubbish, but this is
more difficult. I'm trying to record realities . . . things that
I've really actually positively done and happenings that have
in actuality happened . . . This style I'm using doesn't seem
right at all. 'Wrath broke dot-dot-dot-' etc., etc., etc. It's not
really *me*. If only I was (were?) Holden Caulfield! Then all
my experiences would come out in gritty muscular American
teenage talk. 'Gritty muscular' — that's a mixed metaphor,
Robb. But I still wish I was Holden, with a big big allowance
in dollars.
    (I'm a madman. Holden doesn't exist. He didn't write
'The Catcher in the Rye'. He's the creature of the author,
what's-his-name, Salinger, who's probably a smooth phoney
middle-aged New Yorker who wears those square-lensed
thick-rimmed glasses and lives off his royalties in a big
penthouse apartment with a sultry Raquel Welch type of
mistress.)
    Maybe I should forget style and just write what comes
naturally, Scots words and all. (Scots, Scottish, Scotch —
which of these 'comes naturally'?) If I did, whatever came
out on to the paper would be my very own style and I could
read it back to myself and find out what kind of person I am.
'Le style, c'est l'homme même', as Auld Baldy keeps saying
as he hands me back my English essays, implying . . . I don't
want to think what he's implying.
    I'd better go back to my real-life story and make the style
so muscular it'll compensate for the deficiencies of my actual
physical muscles, if that's possible. So here goes.
    On the by-pass I was getting wetter and wetter and colder
and colder. Suddenly I had a visual of Mother worrying when
she found my cagoule on its hook. But, I reassured myself,
she's used to my 'long walks' after hairy scenes with that man
she married. She knows I'll be back sometime. Just as suddenly, Mother's image was blasted out of existence by a car
roaring up behind me and passing so close the wind and spray
nearly knocked me over. It screeched to a halt and the

nearside door swung open dramatically. Was I in a TV thriller? 'Hey, Andy, c'moan in,' shouted a hoarse voice. I didn't know the voice that knew my name. I stood still. 'Fir Chris'sake, Andy, we've nae time tae waste.' The voice was youthful and excited and urgent.

I started towards the tempting warmth and shelter, but hesitated when the driver revved up the engine noisily and unnecessarily several times. The boy who was holding the door open motioned impatiently. I hopped into the smell of leather and cigars and he crashed the door shut as the car took off, the driver screaming the engine through the gears like a maniac.

As the car surged away, I was able to put together what I had glimpsed as I stepped into it with what I could see now in its dark interior, spasmodically lit by flashes from passing headlights. In the back beside me there was a boy of my own age and height. In the front passenger seat there was another of the same size.

(My own age and height. It depresses me even to write the words, but it depresses the hell out of me altogether when people ask me, presumably for purposes of comparative developmental anatomy, exactly and mathematically what they are. Wallow like this, Robb, and you'll lose whatever muscularity your narrative has. Keep it moving.)

In the driver's seat was a boy even smaller than the other two. He could have been eleven or twelve. It took a moment or two for my mind to register that he was the one actually controlling the car, pretty efficiently, at seventy or more, with the wipers barely coping with the waterfall hitting the screen.

The boy beside me sat leaning forward, his eyes moving from the road ahead to the speedometer. As the needle moved upwards I saw that the limit was at 160 m.p.h., so it was a Jag or a Porsche or even a Ferrari. The boy's mouth hung open and his hand hovered around his flies. Every so often he gave them, or the animal inside them, a good tug. The boy in front switched on the radio-cassette, a quadro-phonic job, and the car was filled with a Stones track that I like a lot and that harmonised with the rush of the car through the night.

I began to yield to the excitement of the moment, as the car's heater thawed me. My eyes too kept moving to that needle as it rose and rose and rose. Pleasure spread from my solar plexus, or thereabouts, but I kept my hand away from my flies. Honestly, I did. Even when the boy in front twiddled the knobs of the radio and lost the Stones, I was not disappointed for long, as the boy beside me had other excitements for me.

'Get the polis. Kin ye no get the polis waveband?' he kept asking. 'They'll maybe be efter us.'

This seemed to egg on the driver, for the needle rose and rose again as he pushed the car beyond the ton. With an ecstatic jerk my companion turned to me, putting his hand on my knee and squeezing hard.

'We nicked a real hot-rod, eh, Andy?' he asked eagerly.

Monosyllables seemed in order.

'Aye,' I ventured.

His hand slid up my leg, knowingly. 'Ye're drookit, man, but we'll be hame in twa hoors an then ye kin have yer wee hairy Mary.'

I took his hand away. 'Poof,' I said, meaningfully.

'Okay, we ken whit you like,' he said, in a puzzled way. It wouldn't be long before he found out I wasn't the right Andy. Then what would happen?

As I write, in my present enforced isolation, I realise that I was no longer worrying about going mad, whatever I'm doing now, crazily scribbling like this. The situation was insane, maybe the other boys too, but at least I was using all the wits I had to cope. I was doing at least as well as Holden would have done.

The two passengers started to talk, but I could make out little of what they were saying. It was all too allusive, slangy, and adenoidal. (Yes, *my* adenoids have been seen to, thank you. What a wimp I am sometimes!) I did pick up that they were talking about some out-of-the-ordinary school they all attended, various boys there, and who were the hardest men. Andy, whoever he was, came from some separate place called 'the unit' where the least hard men were, so I would have to be careful not to speak out of turn. Keeping mum, I just let the thrusting joy of the forbidden speed carry me along.

The others were so engrossed in talking and the driver in listening that none of them noticed huge quadruple headlights behind us. They were gaining on us fast. I turned to look and the boy beside me saw me full-face in the white glare.

'Ye're no Andy at aa!' he cried.

The headlights developed a blue flashing light above them.

'The polis!' I shouted, without thinking and in a passable imitation of their hoarse nasality. I was instantly forgotten in a babble of viciously obscene language. The driver revealed a bass voice and a determination that the police were going to have to work hard to catch him. He accelerated away and I found myself hanging on to the grab handle, urging him on excitedly and yet afraid of injury or death. (Oh, that mindless exhilaration! How I could use it now, in reality, instead of just writing about it, cooped up in this stinking hole, with the walls closing in.)

The chase did not last long. Beyond the end of the dual carriageway the police had set up a roadblock of two landrovers with wide fluorescent stripes on their sides. The driver braked, with a long shriek of tyres.

'Haud on, boys,' he shouted, 'we're gaun through the hedge.'

There was a thud, shudder and heave as the car took the kerb, a moment of ominous quiet as we skidded across the verge diagonally, then a literally sickening jolt and smash of glass as the car came to rest on its side. I found myself lying on top of my companion, dazed from a dunt on the head, seeing stars, and hearing a high singing note. I couldn't move, but he was trying to open the door below him, but it was jammed, of course. As he wriggled desperately to free himself from me and reach the other door, I passed out.

When I came to properly, after being half-aware of voices and lights and being lifted, I was still in my damp clothes and lying on my back under a smelly brown blanket on a bench in what seemed to be a narrow lobby. Looking up at the ceiling blearily and listening to the shrill resonance that was filling my skull from the inside, I knew, without having to think about it, that this was a police station and not a hospital. I knew too that I had to be ready for more unpleasant happenings, like being forced by an unholy alliance of police and parents to return home before I was ready for it. I am not, repeat not, a cry-baby who wants to run home to Mummy. I'm going home in my own time.

I turned my head. Almost within touching distance, on another bench against the drab wall opposite, sat three boys. Two I recognised right away as the passengers from the car, both dressed like me in grotty tee-shirts and clarty jeans. They were red-eyed and down in the mouth and they still needed to clutch at their flies every so often. Their bruised and blotchy faces and their skinny tattooed arms made them almost pitiful. I could handle either of that pair, I thought, undersized though I am, and maybe both together. Andy the

Hard Man. I still can't recall them as separate individuals because the third boy, the driver, grabbed all my attention as
soon as I focussed on him. He was someone byordinar
altogether, black-browed and tiny and fierce, his arms grimly
folded. His studded Levi jacket was ripped from collar to
waist-band, revealing a smooth golden skin and a muscly
shoulder and arm. His jeans had style, stretched tight over
aggressively jutting knees. He was my age, and maybe older,
and not taking defeat easily. Perhaps I wasn't such a hard
man, for I didn't want to tangle with him, ever again. He'd
had three lives in his hands and he'd gambled with them.

Weighing up the place and the three boys had diverted me
from the condition of my cranium. which was still sore and
singing without any let-up. I lifted it, to test my general well-
being, and immediately the dark boy leaned over to me.

'Dinnae move and keep quiet,' he whispered.

I rested my head again.

'Whit's yer name?' he asked.

'Andy,' I whispered back.

'Andy whit?'

'Andy Robb.'

'Listen then. Yer name's Andy MacPhail. That's whit us
three has jist tellt the polis in wir statements. Okay?'

'Robb the snoab,' one of the others giggled.

The dark boy — I never found out his name — turned on
him. 'His name's MacPhail, ya runt,' he said through clenched
teeth. Then back to me, 'Ye're a hell of a man, okay? Ye're
Randy Andy, that sexy ye cannae wait for it, so ye're a per-
sistent absconder.'

I grimaced cagily, my brain flipping through a hundred
options. 'It would be simpler to simulate a memory loss,
wouldn't it?' I asked.

'Smart guy, eh?' He clenched a white-knuckled hard-
looking fist. 'Jist stop talking Englified and say yer name's
MacPhail.'

'Okay,' I murmured, partly because I was in no condition
to resist his threat, partly because some of the illicit excitement of the by-pass was still with me, and partly because I
was going along with whatever would save me from a return
to my family and the barrage of stupid questions they are
bound to ask me about this escapade, or the stony silence
that is just as likely. Mostly, though, I was influenced by the
dark boy's animal magnetism and, yes, his beauty. It was an
effort to write that last word, but no other will do. Compared

to the rest of us, he was a god — one of those ancient ones, half-animal and half-human and all unpredictable power. I had to pay some kind of homage, didn't I?
    The god spoke. His voice was fluty and polite, without a trace of menace. 'Sir, Andy MacPhail is coming round, if you wish to speak to him.'
    Right away a police sergeant appeared by my side. My hackles rose, don't ask me why. 'You are Andrew Stewart MacPhail?' he asked in a phoney English accent. Maybe he thought it sounded official.
    'Mphm,' I nodded.
    'You have just absconded from Balriddie List D School?'
    'Could be.'
    'Not for the first time?'
    'Maybe no.' He was believing me, I could see. How easy it is to keep a lie going, and how satisfying!
    'They're not having you back, if that's a comfort to you. Can you stand?'
    'I dinnae ken.'
    'Stand up then,' he said, whipping off the blanket and yanking me to my feet.
    I saw a star or two to accompany the one-note celestial choir, but stayed upright, hate helping me. The sergeant, blithely unaware of anything I might be feeling, pretended to relax into a Scots accent, but it sounded just as phoney as his English one.
    'Sit doon. Oor doactor said ye'd be okay, but if ye're no ye kin ask to see anither when ye get tae the Assessment Centre.'
    He then read me a short statement, obviously based on what the others had told him, and asked me to sign it. I did so, under the watchful eye of the dark boy, and hating the sergeant even more, for I could see he thought he was pulling a fast one. If he is, I determined, it's one more reason for getting my own back. Somehow. Anyhow.
    He turned to the others. 'Balriddie are comin fir ye in ten meenits,' he said. 'Jist time fir a drag.' He handed round a packet of cigarettes. The god took one, lit it with a fancy lighter and inhaled deep into his lungs. Perhaps he's an Aztec deity, I thought, and is propitiated and controlled by offerings of the sacred weed. There was something ritualistic, a fawning on dangerous power, in the way the sergeant had offered him the packet first. (Budding social anthropologist A. Robb in full flight!) I came last of course and refused, indicating my head.

'Randy's feart that fags'll spile his perfoarmance,' one of
the others sniggered.

I kept a low profile (why do I use clichés?) and said nothing, for I was wondering what an Assessment Centre was.
It sounded sinister, coming from the sergeant, like something
from the Gulag Archipelago. I tried to guess who would be
assessing whom and how it would be done. (If I'm being
assessed now I'm not aware of it. The place feels like a jail to
me.) These thoughts, if that's what they were, were interrupted by hearty voices from beyond the corner of the lobby.
The sergeant disappeared.

'It's the twa beardy screws,' said the dark boy. 'Turn yer
face tae the waa, Andy.'

I did as he commanded, as I had to, and he covered me to
the top of my head with the blanket. I nearly choked with
the foul odour, but the touch of his hands had such authority
I dared not complain.

'They'll no come in here, but we cannae tak chances,' he
said. 'Ye'll mind yer name's MacPhail?'

'Randy Andy, that's me,' I said, seeing a momentary
mental picture of the more interesting aspects of Koo Stark.

'Ye're no bad for an English bastard,' he muttered before
turning away and raising his voice. 'Okay, boys, we're wanted.'

I heard the three of them shuffling out and then the hearty
voices again, with perhaps a hint of anger in their joviality.
Then silence, except for the sergeant shifting his feet. That's
what it sounded like, but he might well have been indulging
in other less innocent practices. I took the blanket off my
face and lay for the better part of an hour while the dunt on
my head throbbed, accompanied by visions of 'A Day in the
Life of Ivan Denisovitch'.

How would Holden have coped? He'd have started, I
thought, by having a long and interesting conversation with
the sergeant, the kind of thing I'm no good at, especially
when I hate someone. He'd have been sorry for him because
of his sad serge uniform and his pitifully polished boots, and
then sick to his stomach with his phoney-ness. And Iain
Crichton Smith, he of the diamond words, what would he
have done? Made a poem? 'Those who move others and are
themselves stone, Should be hated without ambiguity ... '

These literary meditations are a load of cobblers. I'm
making them up, now, as I write. What I was really doing at
the time was trying to comfort myself with thoughts of
Raquel Welch. Hardly a literary pursuit. However, her image

didn't work its usual magic. I was cold, and sort of shrunken, and the night was still young. There was nothing to do but lie there, fight off the Gulag Archipelago and try to hear what was going on round the corner in case it had to do with me. The sergeant seemed to have an ever-increasing stream of callers — I hoped they all hated him too.

In the end, my transfer to this place was effected without fuss by police car. The two policemen who escorted me were impersonal but kindly. One gave me a piece of chocolate (warm from his pocket) when I refused the ritual cigarette. The Centre is actually within this City and Royal Burgh where I have lived all my life, but I didn't know of its existence before. It has massive glass front doors and as I emerged from the car I could see a brightly lit hall, like a hotel foyer. My two escorts and I stood for what seemed like a long time, after one of them had rung the door-bell. Then two informally dressed men appeared, talking animatedly to each other. The bigger one produced a bunch of keys on a long pocket chain and unlocked the front door.

'MacPhail, eh?' he asked the policeman, without looking at me.

'Yes, Mr Scott,' said one.

'Any papers?'

'Just the body.'

'You'll be wanting away?'

Both nodded and turned back to their car. After the big man, Mr Scott, had wordlessly motioned me inside and locked the door he re-started his conversation with his companion, who was a squidgy pop-eyed wee man, while shepherding me across the foyer and into a bare corridor.

I was pretty confused at this point, I must admit. 'No papers' and 'Just the body' and the sound of the key in the lock were echoing in my head. My eyes were dazzled by the bright lights in the foyer and the vivid patterns of the carpet and the huge modernistic prints on the walls and the brilliant covers of the arm-chairs tastefully arranged round unused-looking coffee tables. When we entered the dim light of the corridor I could barely see. But my nose was in working order. It certainly was. The smell of that corridor was a mixture of the sweaty fragrance of the changing rooms at the school playing-field and the early morning aroma of cold deep fat from the cheapest of Chinese chip-shops.

To add to my confusion, Mr Scott's deep voice was reverberating down the corridor. Was I supposed to listen to him?

'I don't care what the policy is, Mister Blaikie,' he was boom-
ing, 'I'm the senior man on duty and I say that this character's
going to be checked in, showered, and bunged into the cooler
in five minutes flat. If the duty-roster says I'm on duty all
week-end, it also says that I hand over to the night man at
ten o'clock, not five past.'

He unlocked what seemed to be a store-room and we all
went in. He seized a large crumpled polythene bag and held
the mouth of it open towards me. 'Pockets,' he said.

I looked at him. I knew what he meant, but this was the
first thing he'd said to me and I was still confused by the idea
that I was going to be assessed. Perhaps the way I behaved
now would be noted down and used against me? Sure enough,
Mister Blaikie was fiddling with a wee black notebook he'd
taken from a shelf. I tried to work out how I should act, but
Mr Scott was in a hurry.

'You know the drill. Move.' I still looked at him. 'One
thing at a time. Into. The. Bag. Mac. Phail. And. It. Will. Be.
In your own interest. Not. To. Try. Any. Funny. Stuff.'

Obviously, my options were: conform and be assessed, or
reveal my true identity and be sent home, so I dropped my
hankie, my house-key and my 3½p into the bag, feeling quite
a sense of loss as I did so. As if they mattered! Mr Scott called
them out to Mr Blaikie, who wrote them carefully into the
wee black book, now revealed as more-or-less innocuous.

'Cigarettes,' said Mr Scott.

'I haven't any,' I said. Mr Scott raised an eyebrow, perhaps
at hearing my accent for the first time. Was he making a mental note of it?

'You'll be desperate. I'll give you one after breakfast,
maybe. It depends, of course.' He was still holding the bag
open to me. 'Clothes,' he said.

Take my clothes off? Was this part of the assessment
too? I stayed not for an answer but conformed again, re-
sponding to impatient gestures from Mr Scott. I stripped
everything off, still damp, right down to my birthday suit.
The process was accompanied by a series of peculiar coughs
and throat-clearings from Mr Blaikie. The store was infernally
cold, but I had to stand there, naked and unmagnificent, while
Mr Scott checked the pockets of my jeans, inserting expert
knowing fingers into them one by one. I began to feel skinnier
and skinnier and pimplier and pimplier. As casually as I could
I covered my private self with one hand, but that didn't make
me, or it, feel any bigger or more human. I felt like an object

with a ridiculous tassel attached to it and hellishly exposed
and raw. I was beginning to think that home might not be
such a bad place after all when, without warning, it happened.
From the inside 'secret' pocket of my jeans Mr Scott
produced a folded and flattened potato-crisp packet. What on
earth, I wondered, forgetting my nakedness, is that doing
here? It was intimately familiar, somehow, and yet in these
surroundings, completely and utterly strange. Not mine, anyway. Nothing to do with me. As Mr Scott peeled off the tape
with which the little bag was sealed my mind went numb, so
that I was neither surprised nor unsurprised when he gave a
long whistle and withdrew from the bag a squashed bundle of
grubby papers. I could see sepia and orange engravings. David
Livingstone. Africans in leg-irons. Mr Scott counted the
papers reverently.

'Potato-crisp bag,' he called out to Mr Blaikie, 'containing
ten Clydesdale Bank ten-pound notes. One hundred. One.
Oh. Oh. Pounds. Sterling.' Then to me, 'All your very own, I
suppose? Earned by honest toil and all that?'

'Well, actually,' I began, unable to say anything rational
and shivering forbye.

'Oh, it's *actually* yours, is it? Your allowance from dear
old Dad, what what?' I wasn't far short of paralysed with the
cold, but I must have nodded. 'In that case, we underlings
will enquire no further. Our betters have to earn their salaries
too, when they condescend to return to duty on Monday
morning. Mister Blaikie, show him what you've written in the
book.'

Mister Blaikie turned the book to me, but kept his distance.

Mr. Scott became sarcastically formal. 'You confirm,
MacPhail, that this entry is correct, correctly dated, and in
ink?'

My head jerked in a shivery spasm which Mr Scott took
for a nod. He proceeded to pull the sleeves of his hairy fake-
Icelandic cardigan half-way up his horrible great hairy forearms and with ostentatious care re-folded the notes, returned
them to the packet and re-sealed it. Then he held the packet
out at arm's length between finger and thumb, glanced at me,
and when he saw I was looking, dropped it into the polythene bag, which he quickly closed with a piece of string.

I was in a dwam, not sure I wasn't dreaming all this, but
Mr Scott brought me to by grabbing a pair of pyjamas from
a shelf and throwing them at me. I whipped on the trousers
p.d.q., followed smartly by the jacket.

'Right, Mister Blaikie,' said Mr Scott, 'you shower him and I'll write him up in the office.' Write me up? My mind was boggling, but Mister Blaikie was wriggling his shoulders and looking at me oddly. 'With these fellows,' he said, 'we're supposed to ... '

'Are we supposed to work more overtime than we'll get paid for?' demanded Mr Scott. 'The Cuts, Mister Blaikie, the Cuts.'

'It's not that, it's ... '

'Oho, *that*'s your problem?' said Mr Scott and turned to me. 'You won't rape him, will you? Tell him you won't. Go on, tell him!'

I managed to convert a shiver into a shrug of my shoulders. What on earth is he going to say in his write-up of me? 'Admitted — one rapist, in possession of £100'?

'You are a rapist, aren't you?'

'So everyone keeps insisting,' I said. 'I seem to be typecast.' That sounds cocky, but I wasn't feeling cocky. Pyjamas are better than nothing, but no real defence. What do I mean? Defence against what? I was wishing the pyjamas had zip-up flies.

'Aye-aye, Mister Blaikie,' opined Mr Scott, 'we're forgetting that he's middle-class. Mid-dle. Class. But it figures, Mister Blaikie. Working-class kids aren't allowed rides in cars, so they have to steal them. Middle-class kids aren't allowed sex, even when they have a hundred pounds to buy it, so they have to steal it. Right, MacPhail?'

I risked shrugging my shoulders again, but Mr Scott wasn't looking. He was going off at full steam — to 'write me up' I was afraid. Mister Blaikie blinked several times, handed me a towel as if it was obscene, and led me to the shower room. His behaviour while I was under the shower was so odd that I can't bring myself to be too specific about it on paper ...

Perhaps I should force myself to write at least part of the truth about Mister Blaikie's antics. After all, Holden was able to describe the perverts he saw from his hotel window. Mister Blaikie didn't move from just inside the door and stood there going very red in the face ... I *can't* be more specific. I really can't. This is Scotland, not New York, and I'm Andrew Robb, not Holden Caulfield/Salinger.

Otherwise, the shower was super, hot and plentiful, and I felt almost human as I dried myself and put on the pyjamas again. Mister Blaikie, his face now a dirty grey, composed himself and led me circumspectly away, up some stairs and along a corridor with huge windows on both sides, like the Aquarium at Edinburgh Zoo. The atmospheric pollution here was different to that downstairs. It smelled like the old Primary Three classroom used to on a wet day when all the kids were steaming damp and half had wet their pants because the headmistress was on one of her rampages and everyone was scared to ask to 'leave the room'. The smell seemed to float on a foundation of floor-polish. Through the reinforced glass of the windows, dimly lit, I could see rows of beds, a tousie head on every pillow that wasn't supporting a skinhead or a punk-head.

I was not exactly reassured by that smell, or those eerie windows, or the sight of all those kids peacefully sleeping. I didn't know if they were juvenile delinquents or mental patients. (Scott and Blaikie weren't wearing white coats or navy-blue uniforms, but perhaps they'd taken them off because they were going off duty?) There was no telling from the outside of the kids' heads what malfunctioning, if any, was going on inside them. If I was assessed as insane nobody would believe me if I insisted that I was Andrew Robb, a case of identity confusion. It's surprising, isn't it, how many thoughts one can think while walking the length of a quite short corridor.

At the end of the corridor was this room I'm occupying. It's not a padded cell, as I'd more than half expected, it's just an ordinary cell, but the staff have phoney names for it. They call it 'the isolation room' or 'the separation room' or 'the cooler'. It would be more honest of them to call it 'the cell' or to use the accurate name its occupants use — 'the slammer'. But perhaps the staff don't want to be honest. Why should they? They're adults.

Mister Blaikie locked me in and I smelled its unique smell for the first time. It can only be described as concentrated essence of gents' public convenience amalgamated with the pungency of the pavements around a pub on a Saturday night before the vomit has had time to dry. The amalgam is sandwiched between layers and layers of disinfectant and something else, which Holden could have described, but I can't. I hardly notice it now.

I looked around and saw a foam mattress and a blanket on a cement platform; a window with obscure glass through which, in daylight, I can just see bars; a ventilator; a toilet buried in a concrete block and with a foot-stud flush; and a judas-hole in the door. Heat, rather too much of it, seems to come from the ceiling. One wall is painted black and a few pieces of chalk kick around the floor so that inmates may draw or write what they fancy, but nobody seems to have bothered. I don't need the black wall because I have this jotter and ball-point that Jimmy brings me.

I should have mentioned Jimmy before. He's the Night Supervisor, a little bald chap with his own ideas, and my link with sanity. My only link with sanity. He came on duty at ten o'clock, I suppose, when the other two went off, but he didn't visit me for an hour or so. When he did I was in the dumps, wide awake and without a trace left of the excitement of the by-pass. My head was hurting like a bastard, I was convinced I was in a mental hospital and I hadn't been able to raise Raquel Welch at all, just when I needed her most. I would say that that woman obsesses me if I wasn't thinking of trading her in for Koo Stark. I'm a madman. I swear it. Being locked up is what I deserve.

Jimmy locked the door behind him and stood looking down at me, making chewing motions. He was wearing a white shirt with the sleeves rolled up, a narrow black tie, baggy black trousers and white tennis shoes. His knotty veiny arms were covered with tattoos.

'Whit's yer name?' he asked, between chews.

'Didn't they tell you?' I replied, with touching faith in 'they'.

'They'll have wrote it in the book, but I dinnae bother wi that. I like tae hear things frae the lads theirsels. Whit are ye cried?'

'Andrew Robb.' Somehow, I *had* to tell this man the truth.

'Oh aye. And whit are ye in fir?'

'I'm a case of mistaken identity.'

'Oh aye. Mphm. Ye'll be wanting a fag?'

'I don't smoke.'

'Oh aye, fancy that.' More chewing. 'Weel, ye'll see me every twa hoors and maybe oftener. But if I keek through the hole an ye're sleepin, I'll jist leave ye. Ye hungry?'

I told him the truth, that the policeman's chocolate was the only thing I'd eaten since dinner-time.

'The bastards,' he said with some venom, and went off. He was back in no time with a piece-box full of bully-beef sandwiches, a packet of biscuits, and an enormous flask of coffee.

'Eat whit ye want,' he said, 'they're ma ain. I've nae dealings wi the kitchen here.'

As I ate, we started the first of the long conversations

which, along with this scribbling, makes the nights bearable,
even enjoyable. Jimmy sits on a chair he brings while I sit
up with my back against the wall. Every so often he goes off
checking that all the doors are locked and that the right tally
of heads is on the pillows. Back with me again, he leaves the
door open so that he can hear the bells — one for the front
door, one for the telephone, one for the fire alarm, and the
only one I've actually heard, which always provokes him.

'They cannae haud their pee at aa, they laddies,' he ex-
claims as he slopes off, fetching his keys out of his pocket as
he goes. (Subtle allusive author Robb leaves the reader to
work out that the boys are locked into their dormitories and
have to call Jimmy if they experience micturition.)

On that first night I asked Jimmy what an Assessment
Centre was and he gave me an old-fashioned look.

'It's jist a Remand Home,' he said, 'but the high heid-yins
decidit tae change the name. It wis whit they cry a "public
relations exercise". The neebours had been complainin.'

This was a relief, but only for a moment. Surely, if I was
sane, I'd have known it wasn't a mental hospital!

'So there isn't any "assessment" then?' I asked anxiously.

'I wadna ken aboot that. The day staff are aye writing re-
ports.' His voice had a certain finality.

I didn't dare to ask more questions, so I was left wondering what sort of a report Mr Scott might write about me.
From the way he talked it would be hostile as well as in-
accurate, like a school report. I'd have been in a high old
state if Jimmy hadn't begun to talk soothingly about his
experiences at sea before, during, and after World War Two.
I cocked my ears for here was real-life, and racy, material
that would be very useful if I ever want to write a sea-story.
Move over, Monsarrat!

Later in the night I told him *my* story, giving him my
address and even the name of the educational establishment
(so-called) which I attend. He believed me, I could see, but was
sweirt to do anything about it, which was fair enough, as I'd
got myself into the place deliberately, almost. When I pressed
him a little, it emerged that he could barely read or write,
hence his lack of interest in 'the book', in which, I gathered,
details of admissions are recorded and in which he is supposed
to write down any happenings of importance. 'If it really
matters,' he said, 'I phone the Officer-in-Charge.'

'Couldn't you phone him about me?' I asked. I was so
enjoying Jimmy's yarns and his relaxing company that I was

in no hurry to get out just then, but I did want to know how
to set about getting out if I began to want to. (Jimmy isn't
here as I write this, so I'm all on edge again. What if there
isn't a procedure for getting out? If there was a Gulag Archipelago in this country, it would be a secret, wouldn't it? Go
back to writing about Jimmy, he's your link with sanity,
remember? If this place was part of the Archipelago, he'd
have told you, surely.)

'He's awaa fir the weekend,' Jimmy was saying, 'the De-
pute's left and there's nae replacement. Scott's Third-in-
Charge an he wadnae believe either of us.' That note of
finality again.

I had no choice but to give up and hope there was some
way out for me, with or without that £100. I refused Jimmy's
offer of a 'tranny' and begged for pencil and paper, which he
went and fetched. He handed them to me with a solemn
warning.

'I'll hae tae tak them awaa in the mornin afore the day-
staff come on. They think ye could damage yersel or attack
folk wi that ball-point. I had tae nick that jotter frae the
class-room.'

It's a good fat jotter too, bless him. If I keep my writing
small it'll last quite a while, and the ball-point is turning out
to be a good discipline (as Auld Baldy would say) after my
usual pencil and rubber.

How it is we've trusted each other so quickly I don't
know, but Jimmy now leaves the cell door open when he's
off on his rounds. He must think I'm sane. He's in a minority.
On my side, I'm absolutely convinced that Jimmy won't let
anyone see this jotter. Which is just as well, for I'm writing
like a madman. I've changed to the present tense, too. I
wonder why? It gives immediacy, Baldy says, but at what
cost? I've been so obsessed that I didn't stop, except for
Jimmy's visits, till after five o'clock on Saturday morning.
Last night was the same and now it's the wee hoors of
Monday morning and I'm still at it. I can't stop. What on
earth would I do if I did? Look at the bare ceiling? Think
about Raquel Welch/Koo Stark for hours on end? Enlarge the
holes in the plaster with my finger-nails, pretending I was
digging my way out? No, no, no, I must go on scribbling and
try to be rational.

Three things are bothering me now. *First*, school tomorrow, or rather today. I want to be there for a reason, a
very special reason, which is now over-riding my reluctance

to go home and face my father's wrath and Mother's insistent anxiety, *Second*, those ten pound notes, if they exist. I can't seem to focus my thoughts about them at all. *Third*, I'm not sure I could take another day here. The nights have been okay because of Jimmy, but the days are hell. The rational thing to do is to try and sleep, but all my attempts are interrupted by an incredible variety of unbelievable happenings, if I may be tautological. (Or do I mean pleonastic? Or just repetitious? I wonder if Jimmy could nick a dictionary too? I'm Andrew Robb and I'm a wordaholic, with irrational lexicophagous tendencies. I need new words like a junkie needs fixes.)

These happenings, they really are insane. They include two-hourly visits by staff in pairs, as ordained by Act of Parliament, according to Mr Scott. Yet Jimmy comes to see me on his own, when he's alone in the building. He must be extra-Parliamentary and sane. But then he would be.

After breakfast I have to scrub the whole cell, bed platform and all, with hot water and disinfectant, though I haven't pee'd or defaecated on the floor. The regulation pair of staff watch me, arms akimbo. I usually get my pyjamas wet, but am told they'll dry.

At tea-time yesterday the meal was brought by a middle-aged woman, escorted by Mr Scott.

'Satisfy your curiosity, Miss Porteous,' he fog-horned, 'have a good look at the answer to many a maiden's prayer.'

'It was you who insisted that I came, Mr Scott,' she acidulated, 'he looks as if he needs a proper diet and a bit of mothering.'

'Haw-haw-haw!' bull-roared Mr Scott and I was left to eat my baked beans off their plastic plate with my fingers. Which did I prefer to be, an undernourished little boy or a sex-fiend? The fiend, obviously. Mothering I need like a hole in the head.

All the time there are noises, some comprehensible and some not. Bawling and banging and stamping. Thrashings-about and whooshings and what sound like throttlings. The last may come from the plumbing — I can't tell. There's no doubt, though, about the horrible screams and even more horrible laughter coming from what Jimmy tells me is the girl's wing, which must be very close by. Worst of all, yesterday the girls found out somehow that there was a rapist in the slammer and started to talk *at* me through the ventilator. Jimmy says they have to stand on the seat in one of their toilets to do it. Some of their remarks are really very crude indeed and made in harsh voices, but others are supposed to be throaty seductive whispers. Luckily the girls' visits to their toilets seem to be rationed, for their talk never lasts for more than a few minutes at a time. If it didn't stop I'd be even farther round the twist.

The way I'm writing about those girls suggests I might be some kind of innocent who hasn't even got a girl-friend. I have one, though. Fat Fiona Phimister my siblings call her, and I'm supposed to lose my temper about the adjective, but I don't bother now because she hasn't been fat for a year or so, only kind of stocky, which suits me as she's never grown taller than me. We have a rather special kind of relationship, perhaps a wee bit unusual in this day and age. I can't believe it, but we haven't been 'out' together yet, or held hands like Holden and old Jane, but we do get together at the church youth club discos, which we organise for the under-fourteens, poor infants, and we walk to and from school and church together, now and then, when there aren't too many others about. We both like the Stones, too, just to be old-fashioned. Best of all, our classes are together for Art on a Monday afternoon so in twelve hours I could be sitting talking to Fiona about this weekend. I could pretend to write out a poem in Creative Calligraphy while she fiddles about with a felt pen pretending to illustrate it. Artless Annie couldn't care less, a typical art teacher.

Fiona is the quintessence of sanity, with a mind like a razor and a sardonic sense of humour. She's better fun than any boy I know. That's no great praise, but I have often wished she was a boy, so that we could be pals and go to each other's bedrooms and blether half the night away. My being a girl would have the same effect, of course, but I don't like to think about that, not since my tits got tender some time back and I lost a lot of sleep wondering what was happening. Then I read something about 'hormonal imbalance in adolescence' and, miraculously, they got better. Any way I think about it (including the awful fear that Fiona's bedroom would smell like my sister's) bedrooms are out. Still, we have this unspoken agreement that neither of us will date anyone else (when it comes to dating), or get drunk, or experiment with glue or drugs, without consulting the other.

I've felt quite sane just writing about Fiona, but after finishing that last paragraph, and wishing fervently that Jimmy would come back soon, I've lost control. Mad thoughts are starting to echo from the walls of this place. What if

Fiona is like those girls in the toilets? Her sense of humour has been pretty crude lately, especially when she's standing at the school gate with a gang of other girls and giggling as the boys, including me, run the gauntlet. I could hate her then. And I really do hate her when she walks past a gang of boys I happen to be with and pretends not to see me. If some smart alec makes a crack about her, as usually happens, she always gives a pert answer, or a dismissive shrug of her backside, or one of those superior smiles which girls are so good at.

My 'muscular' narrative style has gone. I'm describing nothing but the chaos inside my head. My 'stream of consciousness', as Baldy would call it, is muddy, stagnant, and choked with rubbish.

How is Fiona spending the weekend? There's another mad thought. A First XV fellow, a real thick-head I'll call Joe (after bloody Joe 'Room at the Top' Lampton) has taken to going to church for no religious reason I can see and sitting near her. Often right in the same pew, for god's sake. Perhaps the 'unspoken agreement' is all on my side. Come to think of it, Joe's been hanging round her at the disco too, all fourteen stone of him. Perhaps she invited him to come because she's bored with me ... perhaps ...

Jimmy has left me alone for longer than he's ever done. What can be keeping him? If this is the state I get into in the peaceful night, how on earth will I cope with more of those daylight hours, when I can't sleep or wake and scribble? Or with the Officer-in-Charge, when he 'condescends to return to duty' on Monday morning? Which is this morning, in a few hours?

Unlikely though it seems, sleep is overtaking me ...

I've woken up again, the ball-point still in my hand. What will the morning bring? A grilling from the Officer-in-Charge? The police? My parents? Or just the same routine, Gulag fashion?

Fiona ... I nearly wrote down her real name. My name's not Andrew either. Why am I here? Holden never had this kind of problem and he ended up in some weirdo place out West, so what chance have I?

Jimmy, I'll just eat the last of your chocolate biscuits and lie down properly and drop off. This blanket is beginning to smell of me ...

Well, I'm out of that place and writing this on the lab bench in the Physics double-period. Routine first half of

Monday morning, except that writing up my weekend is far
more important to me than writing up last week's stupid little
experiment. What happened in that Assessment Centre is in
the past, so it's back to the past tense and the most muscular
style I'm capable of.

I didn't have much sleep after all, for at three forty-five or
thereabouts Jimmy came in lugging a mattress and followed
by a boy dressed in pyjamas identical to the ones I was wearing. He was carrying a blanket. I leapt out of bed.

'Get back in there,' ordered Jimmy, dumping the mattress
on the narrow patch of floor beside the bed, 'Here's the real
Andy MacPhail.' He turned to my alter ego. 'This is Andy
Robb. He's been mistook fir ye, he says.'

'You'll let me out, then?' I asked, with indecent haste.

'Na, na,' reproved Jimmy, 'I'm only the night man. This
Officer-in-Charge'll sort ye in the mornin.' He picked up this
jotter and the ball-point and my heart stopped beating, but I
had misjudged him, for he added, 'I'll drop this at yer hoose,
eh?'

I nodded, my heart functioning again, but I still wanted
out. The grilling I would just have to take. 'Can't you ring the
Officer-in-Charge ?' I asked.

'Aye. I'll dae jist that, but at seeven o'clock and no
earlier. Aye. And meantime, I'll be checkin on ye baith. Nae
nonsense!' He started to shut the door, I realised that our
chats might be over, never to happen again.

'Thanks for everything,' I said, unoriginally but with feeling. I didn't want him to leave me, I discovered.

'It's been a pleesure,' he said, and locked us in.

So there we were, the two Andies, staring at each other.
We were the same build, near enough, and our hair was
roughly the same length and gingery colour, so the mistake
made by the Balriddie boys was understandable, but I didn't
waste too much time on comparisons. I was worrying about
sharing a small cell with a real sex-maniac. Jimmy, come back!

It turned out that the sex-mania was the least of my
problems. What I had to cope with, first of all, were Andy's
complaints. He was full of them. Full, pressed down, and
running off at the mouth. He complained of having only one
blanket and feeling cold, despite the stifling heat I was exper-
iencing. He resented my having the bed while he had to lie on
the floor, and when I let him have the bed he complained it
was no softer than the floor. He complained bitterly that the
other boys hadn't bothered to come to the rendezvous to

pick him up in the stolen car. He cursed the weather, which had forced him to go back to Balriddie and hide in a cellar near the boiler. He was annoyed that this was the first time he'd absconded and not reached his home town where, if he'd been picked up, he at least knew the Assessment Centre and the staff in it. He kent naebody here and he didnae like it. He'd been found, he complained, breaking into the school clothing store for something to make a bed with. What he'd eaten he didn't say, but it can't have been good for him for he had diarrhoea, which was the second of my problems. Every so often he jumped up and sat on the toilet, girning about his guts as if he was the only one to suffer. The stench was unendurable, but I had to endure it. He didn't seem to have any qualms about defaecating in my presence, or exposing the whole of his anatomy, the skinny git. (My problem is quite the opposite, of course. I'm prone to constipation. I have a constipated personality too, according to Mother. If I have, how come I suffer from (enjoy?) this galloping logorrhea?)

On or off the throne, Andy's voice was high-pitched and saw-edged and I reached the point where I wanted to scream at him to shut up and maybe listen to *my* problems. However, I reasoned that while he was talking I knew where he was and what he was up to. If I talked, I might relax and he might jump me. He did look sinister in the dim of the tiny blue night-light, which was all that Jimmy had left us. But all he did was girn and girn and girn, like a spiled bairn. Every so often I risked a rational word or two, but that seemed to make him even more infantile. He whined that he would have to go back in front of the Children's Panel (I think that was what he called it) which had sent him away, according to him, for one more-or-less innocent incident with a girl.

'Whit d'ye dae when a girl's beggin ye?' he asked, jumping on to the toilet yet again, and cursing the girl's mother, an auld bag wha was on the game hersel, and wha'd shopped him. When Andy went on to moan about his faimly I began to recognise some of his problems. He didnae like onybody at hame; his father was awaa; his mother's fancy-man was a bastard; and his brithers an sisters an the fancy-man's weans aa ganged up on him. He didnae even like his mither much since she tell't the Children's Panel, 'Ach, he's jist like his faither, he cannae keep his hands tae himsel when there's a lassie aboot. He's better awaa.'

He never complained about one thing for long. One

minute he was giving me his views on school, which were
thoroughly well-founded but incoherent, and the next he was
complaining about the lack of money at home. 'It's okay fir
you,' he said, 'living in a big hoose, wi plentya money comin
in an a joab waitin fir ye.'

At this, any semblance of rationality I possessed aban-
doned me and I was engulfed by resentment and infantility,
just like him. What right had he to say that I was rich? My
accent was his only evidence. 'You're not the only one with
problems,' I blurted out, 'my father . . . ' and I told him
more about that Principal Teacher of Guidance that I've ever
told anyone, even Fiona. She knows without having to be
told, anyway. She always *knows*.

'Christ!' said Andy, wiping his bum, 'whit's he like when
he's pissed?'

'He never gets drunk.'

'Hoo d'ye get money aff him then?' pulling his pyjama
trousers up over his anatomy.

'I don't.' (Well, it's true. I don't. Not 'off' him.)

'Christ!' getting under his blanket again.

There was a silence for a while, during which I pondered
the pitiful pittance I receive each Saturday and the miserable
clothing allowance I'm given on the first day of each quarter,
neither subject to negotiation. Watch my father till he got
drunk? I'd wait till doomsday, and beyond.

Andy broke the silence. I wish he'd kept quiet. 'Whaur
did ye get yer hunnerd nicker, then?'

'What do you mean?'

'Ye had a hunnerd quid when ye were brocht here.'

'What on earth makes you think that?'

'I seen it in the proaperty book when auld Fag-fir-a-feel
wisnae looking.'

'You're a nosey bastard.' (It's the first time I've ever
used that word aloud, except when we read King Lear in
class. Honest!)

'An you're a leear wi ten ten-spoats.'

I answered this manifest truth with silence, a reflection of
the empty numbness within my head. As a tactic it worked
very well, as Andy couldn't thole any silence for long. Neither
could I, cooped up in that hole with him and trying to ignore
what my nose was telling me, but I could thole it better than
he could. He began to talk, in a sad voice, about what it was
like to be marked down as a 'sex-offender' by everybody,
everywhere he was sent. I'm sure I heard the sadness because

I've experienced forty-eight hours of the process myself, from lunatics like Scott and Blaikie and mad craiturs like those girls. I believed Andy too when he started to speak of the real extent of his sexual experience. At that time of night in that ghastly slammer, and because of the sad way he described it, it didn't sound too thrilling, up dirty closes and in cold empty houses with girls I'm sure were pasty and spotty and smelly and stupid. It didn't only make me sad, it scunnert me. He was no messenger from the old pagan gods, no Hermes bringing me a gift from Aphrodite or Pan. He was just a poor fellow-human with a little technical information I was grateful for and a muckle load of misinformation I could recognise as rubbish, even with my mind at low torque. As a turn-on his talk was worse than the girls' crudities.

. . . a thick bearskin rug, the flickering light from a huge log-fire, a fragrant golden Raquel drawing me to her . . . that's how I'm going to be seduced, if I don't go mad first . . .

Back to Andy's chatter. The more I think about it the more fascinating and scunnering I find it. Girls, he implied, stated really, exist to give boys dirty thrills and were to be despised for being willing to do it so readily and so often. Yet they were to be feared too, because their short-term willingness was a kid-on and they had long-term plans for trapping you and skinning you of your money, if you weren't wise to their ploys.

. . . maybe I'd shrink away if Raquel stroked my hair . . . I don't really like being touched . . .

Girls, continued Andy, were 'snobs' if they did not give the boys what they wanted . . . Really scunnert at myself now, I began to wonder if these weren't my own disgusting views on girls, and on Raquel Welch and Koo Stark too. Somehow Andy's foetid nearness and our shared predicament made it difficult to separate his views from mine. Fiona, of course, is my *pal* and someone else altogether.

(Thank God I've got my little dictionary with me now. I've moved to the library, so I have access to the Shorter O.E.D. too. 'Foetid' is a super word, but not as apt as I'd hoped. I already knew it meant 'stinking', which we both certainly were, only he ponged more than I did, but I thought it was also the adjective from 'foetus' and would hint, in a clever way, that our nearness was like twins in a womb. What a pity! But it's still a word I relish for its nasty nuances. Foetid.)

Andy and I had another silence, which he found so

comfortable he fell asleep. I was much less comfortable, and
Raquel Welch was fighting Koo Stark for my £100, when
eventually I fell asleep too. The time would be 5.30 a.m. at a
guess.

We were wakened by Jimmy unlocking the door. 'I've
rung the Officer-in-Charge,' he said to me, 'an he's comin
across in ten meenits tae get rid o ye. He's no awfu pleased.'
'What time is it?' I asked dopily.
'Five past seeven.'
'Whit aboot me?' demanded Andy in a squeaky voice.
'Ach, ye're jist routine. He'll hae his brakefast afore he
has a look at ye,' said Jimmy, chewing away and looking uncertainly from Andy to me. 'I'm awaa. Be seein ye,' he said,
and went, leaving me with the realisation that I had lost my
contact with a very shrewd and kindly gentleman, who had
accepted me for precisely what I am (a mad scribbler with
occasional sane interludes) and then given me exactly the
treatment I needed, within the limits of the four walls of the
slammer and of his duty to keep me there. What condition
would I be in without his talks and without this jotter and
that ball-point? It doesn't bear thinking about.

Right away, Andy started to work up some resentment,
sitting up with his blanket wrapped round him. 'I'll maybe no
be here when the Guv comes tae see me.'
'Where would you go?' I asked, pretending I wasn't all
choked up about the imminent arrival of the Guv.
'Hame.'
'I thought you didn't like it.' Rational Robb plays it cool.
'I dinnae, but I've got my pals there, haven't I? You're no
refusin the chance tae get hame. Tae yir Dad an aa.'
Somehow I couldn't tell him that it wasn't home I wanted
either but my one-and-only pal, Fiona. A pal who happened
to be a girl wouldn't be in his book.
Andy's mind, if that's what his head contains, changed
tack in its sudden way. 'I've tellt ye mair than I've ever tellt
onybody. If ye grass on me, I'll come an get ye. An I'll be fir
a cut of that hunnerd quid tae.'
That hundred quid. I'll show him. I grabbed his arm and
twisted it up behind his back. We struggled on the bed, his
string-and-bone versus my string-and-bone, till I pinned him
against the wall. Oh! the relief of action! I gave his arm an
extra twist and he grunted. I waited, thinking he would try to
throw me off, but he didn't. He couldn't move. I was quite

surprised. He's a physical weakling really. I don't know what the girl, or girls, can have seen in him. Perhaps all the proteins in his diet go straight into building up his what-nots, his genitalia. But they don't look much.

'You won't grass on me, will you' I gritted, like a character in a pulp magazine. Robb the Hard Man Turns on the Heat.

'Naw, ya sexy bastard,' he gasped.

'This is just a friendly fight,' I threatened playfully.

'I ken. That's whit I mean by sexy.'

'You've a one-track mind.' I gave his arm another twist.

'Aaargh! Ye cannae deny . . . ' gasp! ' . . . that ye're enjoying yersel.'

'I'm enjoying beating you.'

'That's sexy an aa, stupit.'

I let go his arm, for he was right. I had disgusting stirrings. That's not the truth, Robb, the stirrings were as pleasurable as ever, but their cause was disgusting. Who's a poof now? I wondered, hoping my hormones weren't unbalancing themselves again. How are you supposed to stay sane?

Andy rubbed his arm and grinned at me, the first smile I'd seen on him. 'Got yin tae?' with an unmistakable gesture.

'Naff off,' I said, turning right away from him.

'Okay, okay, forget it,' he said, without malice and with due respect. 'Ye're a harder man than me. If I have tae come an get ma cut, I'll bring a shiv. Christ! ma guts!'

As he hopped on to the w. c. for the umpteenth time, his butterfly brain had another change of tack. 'Kin ye no pit a word in fir me?'

'You've just told me not to grass,' I grumbled, 'and anyway, who'd listen to me?' I retreated to the farthest end of my bed.

'Educated folk like yersel. The Guv here maybe.'

'But you're going to run as soon as you get a chance.'

'Okay, but maybe I'll no rin sae aften if they lay aff me.'

I wasn't sure I'd have the guts to put in a word for myself, never mind for him, but I was saved from further discussion by the sound of the door being unlocked and then slowly opened. My eyes were pretty well accustomed to the dim blue light, so I could see that the man poking his head in was slightly built, grey-haired and grey-faced. He looked from me on my mattress to Andy on the loo.

'Which of you is ah-mm Robb?' he asked in an English voice.

I raised a finger and he muttered to himself, but my ears
are sharp.

'Is sewage really worth all the hassle?' I heard him ask as
he opened the door fully and beckoned to me with a steaming coffee mug. I could make out that he was wearing a grubby
grey track-suit and scuffed grey training shoes. I threw off
the blanket and stood up uncertainly. Why was he talking
about sewage? As if to answer my unspoken question Grey-
face buried his nose in the mug and kept it there, like forever. It must have smelled nicer than the effluvia from Andy's
rotten guts and from me, sweaty and unwashed and rumpled
in the pyjamas I'd been wearing for two days and three nights.
Message received, we're the sewage, over and out.

Grey-face lifted his nose and beckoned again. I walked
out past him, catching a last glimpse and whiff of Andy, still
sitting on the po holding his belly. He grimaced and lifted
one hand in a thumbs-up sign, implying, 'Buddies, mind!'

I signalled back as Grey-face locked the door, muttering
grimly, 'Let's dispose of the sewage!' He tip-toed off down
the blue-lit corridor and past those eerie aquarium windows.
My feet were bare, so I didn't have to tip-toe. The heads on
the pillows looked exactly the same as when I arrived, as if
time had stood still. If it had, the slammer was a dream, a
nightmare.

I've never been so grateful for a double library-period before. There's a good deal of the usual whispering going on
around me, but there's no actual *obligation* to find a partner
and talk, so I'm scribbling away like mad, full of crazy energy.
Underneath, though, I'm exhausted. I'll flop soon.

Barefooting along behind Grey-face I was panicky and
desperate for a pee. Was he the Guv? How could I tell? His
back was bowed and made him look weary and depressed and
sinister, unlike Mr Scott, whose weekend on duty had made
him ever rosier and more cheerful. (Phonies both. Right, Holden?) If Grey-face was the Guv, exactly how was he going to
'get rid' of me, in Jimmy's ambiguous phrase? Back to the
police station to 'assist the police in their enquiries'? That
sergeant would be keen to pin something on me. The £100
would do for starters. Or was it to be a phone-call to my
parents to come and fetch me, followed by a deathly inter-
view, with all sorts of stupid and irrelevant questions asked?
And then back home, to those long and hostile silences? That

short corridor was certainly a place for panic. By the time we'd traversed it, gone down the stairs and reached the store-room, I was in a fair old froth, my bladder so full I was ready to pee the pyjamas.

Once inside the store, Grey-face locked the door, found my polythene bag and gave me my still damp clothes one by one, wearily ticking off each item in the wee book before handing it over. Needless to say I put them on with the utmost speed.

'Sorry they're ah-mm moist,' he said, 'but the drier's on the ah-mm blink . . . things fall apart, you know . . . '

An apology to the sewage, I thought apprehensively, whatever next? Keeping quiet is the best plan when adults say they're sorry. You never know what they're up to. He gave me my hankie, my key and my 3½p and then held up the crisp packet, looking in the approximate direction of my face. 'Jimmy tells me you attend the seat of learning known as . . . ah-mm?' and he named my school.

'Yessir!' I said, acting the perfect schoolboy.

'You'll be sitting A Levels?'

'Highers in Scotland, sir!' It came out automatically.

'Ah-mm, Highers, quite so.' A suggestion of frost reminded me not to get cocky. 'Which "Highers" are you sitting?'

I told him politely, but I'm damned if I'll write them down here. The Scottish Education Department computer has stored them in its data-bank already. I hope it gets maggots in its mainframe, and syphilis in its software!

'Quite the little ah-mm polymath?' I kept my mouth shut. 'This address you gave Jimmy, is it ah-mm?'

'Yessir!' He had my name and address! Jimmy had grassed. Or done his duty. Whichever, I was now standing to attention, overdoing the rigidity out of panic and the need to hold on to my pee. He could look up the phone-book. He could . . .

'Ah-mm, very residential. Very popular with the ah-mm professional classes. No sewage in evidence.' He paused, then spoke very fast. 'There'll be no need to enquire into this, then?' meaning the £100 inside the packet he was still holding up.

My head jerked like a puppet's and he handed over the packet so quickly it was like a conjuring trick. Almost as quickly, for I was hampered by my agonised bladder, I put the thing away without opening it. I could feel that the notes were still there, though. I'll just lose it somewhere, I decided.

From the store Grey-face took me to an office just off

the foyer. It would be his, I suppose, if he was really the Guv. He sat me clammily on a hard chair, sighed, walked to the desk and laid down his mug, now empty. Then he looked out of the window, where a dank football pitch could be seen in the dull light of dawn. He sighed again, like the End of the World is Nigh.

I vowed I was going to write about reality and not phantasy, but if I write down what Grey-face actually said at this point it'll read as if I'd made him up out of my own fevered imaginings, influenced by my screaming bladder. And how can I describe the faint but unmistakable sensation I had that I might be the sane one, confronted with his mournful maunderings?

'New problems,' he was saying, still looking out of the window, 'why did I ever think "never a dull moment"? New problems are as deadly as old problems. This place is a stagnant pool, with raw ah-mm sewage *swilling* in one end and untreated sewage ah-mm *oozing* out of the other. Every so often a filthy great bubble bursts and there's a splash and a stink in the papers. Then it's back to festering stagnation again. Why don't I break out? There must be a New Life ... back down ah-mm South ... a new squaw ...'

I stayed on the edge of the chair, ready for anything. He went mumbling on and on, dropping his voice till I couldn't hear him at all. The wastepaper basket was next to my chair and I was thinking of dropping the crisp packet into it when he turned away from the window and spoke audibly, 'Back to sewage disposal.'

'Sir?'

'Will your parents have reported you ah-mm missing?'

'It's highly unlikely,' I answered. Report me missing? You don't know my parents! 'Sir,' I added hurriedly.

His grey countenance lightened for a second or two, then darkened again as he returned to looking at the football field.

'You realise that I have no obligation ah-mm whatso*ever* to inform them of your sojourn in the sewage here?'

'I suppose not, sir,' I said, trying to sound neutral while my hopes dared to rise a little.

'Will you be ah-mm *discussing* where you have been with them?'

'Oh no, sir.' *Discuss* with my parents! That'll be the day! 'We don't communicate at that level, sir.'

His face brightened again and he became conspiratorial, almost chummy. 'I should warn you that the police have no

ah-mm glad feelings about your signing that ah-mm ... '
He lowered his voice to a whisper. 'I'd keep out of their
clutches if I were you. Otherwise ... ' and he made a lugu-
brious throat-cutting gesture.
'I'll do that, sir,' I said, my hopes rising further.
Grey-face now picked up a paper from his desk, holding
it as if it was impure. He handed it to me and I found it was a
hastily typed statement that my being locked up was entirely
my own fault. He asked me to sign it, leering greyly. Should I?
I couldn't think clearly. I couldn't think period. Fiona, with
her analytical mind, would have known straight off what to
do. Holden would have used his world-weary wisdom. But
me, I'm muddled, even if sane compared to Grey-face. I
looked up from the paper and he was drooping there, holding
out a pen.
'You'll let me out?' I asked, without meaning to.
'Ah-mm, yes, provided ... ah-mm ... '
I realise now that he'd probably have gone down on his
knees to have me sign, but at the time I was in such a tizzy
that I thought I was in the supplicant's position. Obediently,
I signed. Suddenly, Grey-face was full of energy.
'Terribly terribly sorry about all the sewage nonsense, my
dear chap, but Monday mornings are absolute hell, aren't
they?' He thrust some small change into my hand. 'That'll do
for your bus-fare.' He rushed me out of the room and across
the foyer to the front door. He unlocked it smartly and fresh
air and freedom poured over me, reminding me somehow
that Andy was still locked up in that black hole. Loyalty
matters to me — let the trumpet sound! — and I had half-
promised to put in a word for him. This would be my only
chance. I stopped in the doorway, mustering courage.
'Sir!' I said, 'Andy MacPhail, sir.'
'NO! NO! NO! A complaint about him would really make
my day. What did he do?' No ah-mms now.
'No complaint, sir. I ... '
Grey-face briskly shoved me out of the doorway and almost closed the door. 'What then, if you've no complaint?'
he asked through the crack.
'He's being driven crazy by ... '
'Good god, man, aren't we all? Don't you want your
breakfast?'
'Yessir, but, sir ... '
'Look here, Robb, I have twenty-five other boys, all saying
sir! sir! sir! and not meaning it, and ten fornicating girls, all

trying to seduce the boys.' His face was darkly flushed and his eyes glared redly. 'Grey-face' indeed! 'MacPhail's not my fornicating responsibility at all.' He paused, then added, like a rapier thrust, 'Nor is your fornicating hundred pounds.'

I could only stand like a zombie while he locked the door and strode away manfully on the balls of his feet without a backward glance at me through the glass. Eventually I turned away, the 'fresh' air just plain cold and raw, and freedom, as it turned out, nothing but one disaster after another.

It's Friday evening and I've locked myself in my room with no intention of coming out till I have to. I've stocked up on coke and crisps and I've 'borrowed' a can of bully-beef and some bread and butter.

As I said, my release from the Assessment Centre was followed by a catalogue of disasters. They have been so frightful that I'm not sure I can write about them at all. I'm terrified, too, that more may be on the way. So if I'm going to write anything I must discipline myself somehow. De la discipline, camarade!

Perhaps it would help if I made an actual catalogue of the disasters, with annotations and comments. Mother reckons that if you make a list of your troubles you'll find that two-thirds of them don't really exist — I wonder where I come on her latest list? If I'm no trouble to her, I don't exist, do I?

Firstly, I was caught peeing in that bus shelter by Mrs Brown, the dinner lady I've known and liked very much all my school career. When I left the Assessment Centre I was bursting and there was nowhere but this empty shelter with a big graffiti sign saying PEE HERE and an arrow pointing to the corner. Mrs Brown isn't a lady to keep her mouth shut. I like her, but does she like me? She didn't say anything, but she looked really shocked.

Secondly, my family, always a disaster area, but worse than ever now. What they've done, all of them, is to pretend that nothing has happened; that I was not absent for three nights; and that I didn't turn up on Monday morning looking rumpled and unwashed and ghastly. There have been no stupid questions; no stony silences either. Father banters heavily as usual, Mother worries as always, sister criticises and brother is okay except when sister is present and then he joins in her criticisms. Nothing has changed. No one has taken any notice. I have what are called, I think, 'feelings of unreality'. I could use a kid sister like Phoebe.

Thirdly, Fiona. (It's much easier to write that pidgin-Gaelic pseudonym than her real and much more beautiful Greek name.) When I met her at school on Monday morning she was furious with me for not being at the disco on Saturday. The kids had got out of hand and they really needed a man (me!) to control them. Joe was there but isn't a man, it seems, despite the latest rumour that someone's named him in a paternity suit. Fiona looked so beautiful in her anger that I now get a pain every time I think of her, a real physical pain, like indigestion, and that's not a joke, it's not even remotely funny. I can barely breathe, let alone write, when I remember her dark eyes glistening, surrounded by those fabulous eye-lashes, so long they might almost be false, which they're not. And she regards me as, insists that I am, a man!

Fourthly (after a long gap when I couldn't write at all), this jotter. The only non-disaster that has happened is that Jimmy dropped it through the letter-box in a plain brown envelope addressed in shaky block letters. That was on Monday morning. However, I've been owing Auld Baldy an essay for weeks and when he saw it on my desk on Monday afternoon he just assumed it was my essay, grabbed it and took it away to mark. There was nothing I could do but wait till he gave it me back this afternoon. Here is his red-ink comment, complete with the alliterations he criticises when I use them:

> 'I must say I find your use of Scots and slang words scarcely apposite, your obscenities and profuse profanities profoundly distasteful, and your delving into depravity deeply disturbing. I cannot accept this as an assignment for assessment and must insist that you show it to your Teacher of Guidance. He may be able to help you in ways that I cannot. (Incidentally, the "diamond words" you attribute to Crichton Smith, whoever he is, are a misquotation from Shakespeare. Always check your references.)'

Fifthly, Holden. With my jotter in Baldy's keeping, I found I couldn't write at all, so I tried to re-read 'The Catcher in the Rye' — for the fourth or fifth time I reckon. I tried for three nights running, but I just couldn't read it. Holden isn't like me at all. For one thing, his style is so *consistent*, while I have trouble keeping the same style going for more than a page or two. For another, he's so *cool* about girls, while I have this *burning pain* every time I think about the only girl who matters. Maybe I'm in love. If I am, it's something neither Holden nor Salinger warned me about, the idiots.

Sixthly, Raquel Welch/Koo Stark. I can't raise them at all. Every time I try to, I see Fiona's dark hair swinging as she turned her angry back on me — I smell its clean dark scent too. I suppose it isn't a disaster to have got rid of those two baggages (who have no scent of course) but there's no *comfort* in my thoughts about Fiona.

Seventhly, Andy MacPhail. I feel bad about not being able to help him, but the feeling is wearing off, to be honest. The disaster is that I can't stop wondering what he meant by calling Jimmy 'Auld Fag-fir-a-feel'. At first I thought he was referring to Mister Blaikie, but now I've realised that Jimmy was the only adult in the building when Andy was admitted. Jimmy a queer? I don't believe it! But Andy was street-wise ... I'm confused. Maybe it's a nickname for Night Supervisors? I may never know.

Eighthly, that money. It's still the same old disaster/mystery. I haven't checked to see if it's still in my jeans because I've stuffed them as far behind the wardrobe as I can and then piled old magazines on top. Mother may find them at spring-cleaning time. If she doesn't, where will they be?

Lastly, this diarrhoea. I probably caught it from Andy and I've had it all week. As it wasn't improving, I went to the doctor earlier this evening. To cut a long story short, I emerged from the surgery with a prescription for the squitters and an appointment to see a shrink. The doctor says my parents needn't know unless the psychiatrist insists, and even then I can just opt out of the treatment if I want to. So I'm in the same boat as Holden. Who doesn't exist. Yes, he does, for I'm hanging on to Holden in my head, and sod Salinger.

What am I going to tell the shrink? That I accumulate money and can't account for it? That I'm prone to inexplicable disasters? That I'm wishing I was out of here, away from the pains I get when I think about Fiona, and back on the by-pass under the leadership of the dark boy-god? With his charisma and my brains we would soon be running a real outfit, dealing in thousands in Swiss bank accounts and not tens of tenners in crisp bags. Then I could go and find Holden, my Holden, in Ernie's night-club, if he's been let out of that what's-it place. Most of all, though, dear shrink, I'd like to be back in the slammer, in the middle of the Archipelago, safely scribbling away and with half an ear cocked for Jimmy, dear couthy conscientious Jimmy, padding along the corridor with his piece-box and his flask. How much madder can I get than that? You tell me.

IAN MORRISON

THE CALVING

As he came within sight of the farm the dogs ran across one of the last unploughed parks to meet him, soaking themselves in the deep puddles that lay after the unexpected rain. He fended off their welcoming to keep his school clothes clean then ran the last distance home with them on either side contorting themselves to face him and barking in their excitement, their tails whipping his legs. The untarred road was muddy and the smell of the red clay was sharp and colours fresh and clean after the rain. The sun shone. He laughed aloud as he ran. School was finished and tomorrow would see him begin his summer work weeding the turnip field behind the house. He was not paid for working and his father took it for granted that he would work but for doing this the farmer had promised him another labrador, one from his newest litter. He had been promised that he would get it sometime during the next few days for the farmer knew he worked hard and trusted him to finish the job after being paid. He was a very fine old man, nicer than his own grandparents, though his son was a shite as his own father had said. He knew the work was no more than an excuse to give him the dog, he'd winked and given him a small park to weed that wouldn't take long at all. In the fine weather coming it would hardly be work. He would tan a dark brown and as his hair grew long his parents would moan as they already had about his having another dog and compare him with something from an art college. But during the summer he could always enjoy their disapproval. He saw the dark clouds coming over from the Grampians and felt the closeness in the heat and a huge energy gather within himself ready for the summer. The letter he had been told to give his parents interested him no longer. Everything was silent except for himself and his dogs and their shouts and barkings roared together around the bright farmyard as they ran through it up to the house.

His father was at the kitchen sink, a big man, overweight, rubbing Swarfega onto his forearms as high as the elbows. His mother had been baking girdle scones on the Rayburn. Both windows and the door were open but the heat of the place felt formidable even from the doorstep. His father heard him scrape the mud from his soles and called out, Aye, over his shoulder. He walked in and said Hello, quietly, and buttered one of the warm triangular scones. The scroll of butter nearly melted before he spread it. Ye should cut yir scone in two, said his father. Aye I know, he said, and he spread the top with rhubarb jam and put it on a sideplate and walked through the sitting room to the stairs. He ate it as he climbed to his bedroom then looked out his old clothes and began to change.

His father was fine enough but in a pernickety way now that he hadn't been. He didn't like the Mearns, he knew, its folk to him mad wi siller, and would cross back over the Cairn but for the low wages he'd broken from. Most of his friends were still there, he'd made few here, and he was probably unhappy. He stopped undressing momentarily. The scale of the thought and its suddenness left him in awe of himself.

He could remember travelling in the car with his mother and father, and always to new places; once to Dunnottar Castle. It stood on a high rock that was almost an island and could only be reached by climbing stairs and a narrow steep cobbled road that led through two low tunnels. The wind had cut into them, there were no outer walls on top of the rock, and there had been the massed screams of hundreds of seagulls. The walls had dripped and the rooms had not been paved and lit as they were in the other castles he had seen since. He had thought that he would have loved to have lived there with the knights and the Crown Jewels and the Roundheads outside the walls. From a tower he had looked out over the sea. His father had taken him to the edge of the rock where he had lain down with his head peeping over and only then heard its deafening roar. He had seen its depth, and been madly happy with its power, and had laughed out loud until his father had shouted at him to stop. People had been watching. That was all when he was wee. He remembered walking around making up stories in his head about sieges. He'd been reading a lot then about Robert the Bruce, and Ivanhoe. He slowly pulled on his jeans and his thick knitted boot socks. He still imagined stories, too many now, but there were no other books at home. He floated battleships which were bits of stick in the farmyard puddles and dive-bombed them with pebbles and finally, his patience always exhausted by their buoyancy, he smashed them with his

walking stick. He saw himself blush as he remembered being
rowed at once for the mess this had made of his school trousers
but he could never imagine anything else he could do. His
parents did not seem to understand his need for books, nor
his hatred of visiting the relatives they now did nothing but
visit. They treated him like a six year old, giving him orange
squash and asking him about school and oohing at his marks
then liking him to be quiet, no wonder all his cousins were so
silent and daft.

He sat down on the edge of the bed and saw himself in
the mirror dressed in working clothes that were still marked
with dirt from the week before. His mother was not so fastid-
ious about what he wore at home, and besides the dirt his
clothes were also loose with wear. But at least he did not
have to worry about dirtying his stiff school clothes for two
months. His mother shouted up at him that his supper was
ready and he went down to the kitchen. His parents' faces
were reddened by the heat. His mother smiled at him and
said Ye'll be right pleased yir finished then and he smiled for
he knew he was really even though he knew he would probably be bored by the end of the summer.

During supper his father told them of the day's goings on
at the farm, which as usual seemed to be a series of swearing
matches with the farmer. When supper was nearly over he remembered the letter he had been told to give them and ran
upstairs to get it. His mother read it aloud. It was a list of
books with a note asking that they should be bought for him,
as he shows great promise and a keen interest in literature,
and I think he should be encouraged. Understanding now, he
ran upstairs again to bring down the two books the teacher
had given him herself. He saw himself red faced in the mirror.
He showed his parents the books, heavy leather bound editions
with thick pages, then read out the list picking out the books
he himself would like to read. They had smiled at the letter,
pleased and proud, but when he tried to explain why he only
wanted certain books they became worried and even seemed
a little shy of him. Fit's wrang wi the books yir teacher's
lookit oot for ye, like? asked his mother. He hesitated. He
knew what he should say, that he had read books by people
on the list which he hadn't liked, that the titles of some
sounded daft or boring, that he knew some were about things
that he didn't much want to read about; but he was sure that
those reasons would only annoy them. They would just think

he was being cocky. So he said the first thing that came into
his head, that he wouldn't be able to read all of them. It did
not sound convincing at all, and his father eventually only
agreed to see about ordering them from the Laurencekirk
newsagent. He doubted somehow if it would get as far as that.

A car drew up outside and its horn sounded. His father
slowly got up and went to the window, said Aye, it's Donaldson, and went out to him. Through the open door he heard
them talk. The old vet and his father spoke about the weather
and the ploughing championships which it had just been
announced were to be held at Drumnagair. The finest o grun
there, his father said, nae a steen. If they cannae ploo straight
there they'll be gey poor ploomen. He was cheery using farm-
ing words which took him back to the past and the crofts he
and his mother grew up on. It was a time they always spoke
of. His father said he remembered best the taste of brose and
how he had had to snare rabbits for the family to live. He
finished his tea, he and his mother not speaking. With the
back of his hand he tried to scatter the flies which were landing on the table.

His father came back into the kitchen. The vet followed
him after scraping his feet clean. Margaret he said to his
mother from the door, who laughed and welcomed him in,
and then to himself he smiled and said Well min, that's you
finished wi school for the summer. Aye he said. The vet
laughed and cried out Christ he's getting himsel a rare Mearns
accent and sat down at the table. He was poured a cup of tea
and told to help himself from the table. He took a scone and
told them about the farm sale over by Fordoun. It's a good
buy for Watson, he said, the pipeline'll be through there soon
and he'll get himsel a fair bit off the Gas Board. It's nae right
that one man should hae as much land tae himsel though, his
father said. I wis speakin to the cattler ower it the Dykelands
the ither week an he wis sayin that a the land between there
an Fettercairn belongs tae three men. Damn the bit said the
vet. That land belongs tae the people o Scotland, his father
said. He knew his father wanted some of his own. Aye, you're
right enough, said the vet. Well, the lad that owns this bit'll
be wantin us. Can I use your loo? He went upstairs. There's a
coo calvin at the haim fairm, his father said, an Jocky's sick
again. Och, not again, said his mother. He'll hiv tae get
somebody else, you'll nae be fit tae calve beasts at twa fairms.
Aye, maybe so, bit then I've nae say in the maitter. Bed the
court til I get back, his father said to him, number 89'll be

calvin thenight. She's in the paddock ready, so jist tak her in eence you're finished.

Aye, he said.

His father went off with the vet. His mother began clearing the table, and he stepped out and sat on the doorway to put on his boots. The sun had suddenly been overcast by the dark clouds. Two car horns sounded on the road, and before he could get down to the byre another car drove up through the farmyard towards the house. He recognised it and happily waited on the doorstep.

Brian said that some boys they knew in Inverbervie had gotten a team together and were keen for a game. Most of them had been in the school team they had beaten three weeks ago. But he knew that he could not go. You can play inside right, like Strachan, Brian's father joked. No, he explained, he had work to do. But next week. His mother stayed indoors as they talked. They arranged for Brian to be driven out some afternoon in the next fortnight, and he smiled at that. But he thought as they drove off of how much his father would hate having someone wandering over his farm liable to break or interfere with something. His mother came through from the milkhouse with the smallest zinced pail. Ye could fill this while you're doon there, she said, her voice and her face stiff. He told her about the game next week. Ye'll nae be ga'n if ye're nae tae be back afore it's dark, she said. He walked off down to the byre without a word.

He raged to himself all the way about his parents. He was hardly given room to breathe. Their ways from being brought up on hard little crofts never changed. He thought of his pals, they enjoyed the record players and the BMX bikes and the computers now that he couldn't afford and had no hope of being given. Christ. We've still got our own cow when everyone else has enough sense to drink pasteurised milk and we've that bloody range that takes hours to clean, and no TV, and I suppose I'd better get down on my knees sometime and thank Christ we've running water for the bog. And we never go anywhere. He had been hoping that there would be a trip to Aberdeen promised to get the books. He would read them if he got them. He had nothing else to do when the weather stopped him working and hardly anyone ever came out to see him, he was too far out in the wilds. And when they did he'd always work to do. And his parents didn't trust his pals, not since they'd met Brian buying a Mayfair from the Laurencekirk newsagent. Jesus, there was no getting to them.

His spirits rose only when he heard his dogs dash down barking behind him.

The byre sat slightly below the level of the yard outside, a ribbed concrete ramp leading down to its concrete floor. He bedded one quarter of the byre with fresh straw, the quarter cornered off by two long gates, then went out to take in the cow. He led her through by a rope halter, which he tied to one of the gates, then stood leaning on the other side of that gate watching her. Her water had broken. She was small but enormous with calf. She's too small, he thought suddenly, and the calf won't be lying properly inside, they'll have to take the machine to her. He thought of what that was like, always, his father pouring with sweat and veined as he cranked and the cow's low moaning echoing in the byre, trapped by the low corrugated iron roof. Bastard Charolais bulls. They meant big calves but they killed too many cattle. He remembered the bad calving last year, a Caesarean during a cloudburts when the rain had hammered on the roof as though it was meant to be smashed.

Fit's this, wee man, gotten her ready? Fine stuff. It was the farmer's son, drunk, with a pal who was drunk as well. The dogs stood silent on one side, their tails slowly twitching. By Jesus, we'll hae fun wi this ane, eh Jim? His she broken her watter yit? His face was fat and sappy and his pupils did not seem the right distance apart. Aye. Ah weel, get the tractor fae roun the side, Jim. There's a chein on the back o it. He took off his jacket and rolled up his shirtsleeves.

His father and the vet returned as the rain was starting to spit. They saw first the tractor being reversed down into the byre and hurried to see what was going on. Then they saw that the farmer's son had the calf's back legs out from the mother as far as the knees and had laid the machine aside and was tieing a bright new aluminium chain round the calf's ankles. The vet saw the boy standing to one side with his dogs, ashen faced. Well min, he called to him. He thought he looked traumatised. He turned to the farmer's son and said, Yir father telt me I'd be as well coming here as well, seeing as yourself and I have aye had bother wi this one. Awa tae fuck man, the drunk shouted, I telt ye last mart I'll be hanlin the calvin here wi the cattler. That right Jim? And he laughed. His pal was tieing the chain through the bogey hook of the tractor. Their breathing rose in clouds. Yir nae daein this wi ony o my cattle said his father, his voice shaking. Your cattle my erse, he shouted. Start her up.

The tractor engine engaged. The vet, slimmer and quicker than his father, leapt onto the footplate of the tractor and with the side of his clenched fist punched the button which killed it. He looked straight at the man called Jim, who had made no move to stop him, then turned to his father. I think the lad might be better off back haim, he said. His father agreed. He turned to leave the byre, feeling very ashamed, the dogs running home ahead of him. But before he had reached the door a violent argument began and the tractor engine was engaged again. There was an appalling echoing noise, and turning round he saw the cow's knees buckle. The calf lay on a patch of stained straw with its spine cleanly snapped and its carcass torn nearly in two.

He had gone straight up to his bedroom and from his window had seen the two cars drive off and his father come walking slowly by moonlight alone up to the house. Now he stood by the open bedroom door feeling all the same only a slight curiosity about what he was to hear. He doubted if it could make him feel sympathy for his father. He had been weak.

He wanted nothing more to do with farm work. That he was sure of. Never again. His two dogs would do, he didn't need a third. They would spend the summer walking the hills as they had done and walking down Drumtochty Glen watching the swans on the loch. And he was going to have those books, and he'd have more from the library, they could object if they liked. They would be on the floor and the chair and on the dressing table piled so high he'd only be able to see half of himself in the mirror. And he would read the lot. Anything but have to do with this place again.

He heard the kitchen door closed. Fit happened? his mother asked, the loon went straight up til his bed wioot a word. He heard his father sit down in his chair and tell her what had happened. His mother gasped. Killed the mither is weel. His father's voice was very quiet and low. There was a long silence. At last, his mother asked, Fit'll ye dae?

The phone rang and eventually his father answered it. From his tone of voice it was obvious from the start that it was the farmer on the line.

Aye? Aye that's right, Donaldson telt ye right. Aye, weel, it bloody sickened me tae. There's never been onything like that thenight. A long silence. I'll tell ye fit I'm daein, I'm changin ma notice. Ye kin hae a week raither than a month. Ach, nane o that, fur fucks sake. I've nae worked here for near enough five year wioot sortin oot you in me heid. You'll nae buy me. You jist gie me ma references and I'll sort oot a float for the flittin, and ye can get that young shite tae clear up his ain mess in the mornin. He'll hae that letter here wi him. His father put the phone down and closed the door to the sitting room behind him. He closed his door, undressed and went to bed. He could not wonder where they would be moving next or in what way he would miss this place, or what would happen if his father couldn't find another job. His disgust of his father had gained enough momentum for him to feel bitter now about not having been told of the move to come. How could they think of keeping such a silence? Did they already have another place fixed up? Did they not trust him to know? He felt vaguely ashamed of his feelings but all the same he lay in the silence of the room and felt his disgust carry everything before it as he lay listening to the roar of his own breathing.

J. C. Q. STEWART

SNOWBERRIES

Look how these berries fling
in their baubles of thick milk on twigs
the green seeds globed in white
which are gliding past like stars
while above the snowberries the tougher skinned
urgent rushing elders go glowing in points
— how knowledge seeds in the flesh or goes to seed.
Why all that welling red juice if not
for some beguilement, and so it is:
between the darkness of this possible wine
and the pure white ballooning of poisons
thing splits from image, knowing from supposing
that if feeding on rareness kills,
from grosser purities, ripely toxic, turn
to all those dark particulars that bunch
like worlds on one stem.

DAVID KINLOCH

BERRIES IN HOLYWELL GRAVEYARD

The cat discovers a continent
and calls it deadberry land,
paws deep to find the furry heads
of old milk-givers and purrers curled there.

With the stealth of a pirogue
he prowls the cypressed creeks
looping strange landing stones
clawed by still settlers
of the humid earth.

From the great god shorn
of his discretionary leaves
blood congeals around
decapitated clusters:

these tiny headberries
flame the night like bloodshot eyes,
'Keep into the kerb' they cry
'or drop like us into deadberry land';
only the cat walks there.

STANLEY ROGER GREEN

SNAKE IN THE GRASS

It lay dozing in a coil,
Like a centrifugal idea
That had lost momentum,

When we startled each other;
Myself, into fascination,
The adder into vivid rage.

Its tiny tongue flickered
Wicked lightning warnings:
I stood stiller than a tree.

Then it stretched, shook out
Languorous folds of itself
And slithered under ferns.

Now I understand Eve's fall:
For what maid born of man
Could resist such brazen eyes,

A masterful solemnity,
A sinuous sliding promise
Of intricate designs?

What wench could feign deafness
To blandishments that oozed
From a honeyed perilous tongue?

And Adam, the plodding crofter,
Busy with compost, had forgotten
All Eve's favourite songs.

IAN J. RANKIN

VOYEURISM

A crisp October day it was when the nun fell from the sky
and landed at his feet. He had been sitting all morning in the
small, badly-lit office, listening to the telephone answering
machine's messages of the night before. He gripped a pencil
in his left hand, though there were few names and addresses
to be noted. He knew the rules of the game well enough by
now not to expect anything else. Soon he tired of hearing the
ritual: telephone rings, activates machine, Jill the secretary's
voice.
    'Hello there.' (Coy, sexy. The reality was oh so different:
forty-five, bovine, married to a brute of a coalminer.) 'If
you've phoned this number then you must have seen one of
our advertisements in your local newspaper. We are J & J
Videos Limited, a family-run concern whose aim is to bring
you the very best in uncensored adult videos.'
    And so on, even featuring a few seconds' recording of
some grunting from one of 'our select choice'. Then:
    'If you would like to receive our catalogue, absolutely
free and with no commitment, sent discreetly under plain
cover, then simply leave your name and address when you
hear the bleep. I look forward to dealing with you soon.
Bye-bye now.'
    Then: bleep, a pause, total silence, the line goes dead.
The man on the other end has had his cheap thrill, but hasn't
the guts to speak into a machine, hasn't the guts to reveal his
identity.
    That happens often. Out of seventeen calls he gets five
names and addresses: three from the Midlands, one from
Glasgow, one from London. On two occasions a name has
been half-uttered before the shaky voice has packed in and
put down the receiver. He smirks at those, rewinds them and
listens again.
    So, five potential customers for whom he must write out
five envelopes, fold and push a cheaply reproduced catalogue
into each, stick down and post. Then home for his lunch.
What a job. He looks around the back office, the walls of

which are resplendent with faded pictures of old football
players torn out of boys' magazines. Ironical that. On a table
sits an unsteady pile of videos in their sleeves. 'Hot Stuffing',
'Geisha Frolics', 'Wild Vixen Party 2'. He smirks again at the
dreadful titles. When he had first started the job, the real
perk had been to slot one of these video cassettes into the
recorder, sitting back to view the wares.

But no longer a perk. Sometimes friends or associates will
want to spend the afternoon in the back office watching a
skin flick. When they do, his face wrinkles with anticipated
boredom, tiredness in his fingers as he pushes home the de-
sired cassette. His boss, too, is tired of the whole thing. For
him, the tapes are merchandise to be distributed, the money
collected and put into the bank, a wife and two sons at home
with the evening meal before him and normal lives to be
lived. To him, the tapes are Christmas toys, slabs of butcher-
meat, supermarket-shelf biscuits. They used to be other, but
that was long ago.

By twelve, he has licked shut the last of the sour envelopes
and has taped them all for further security. He shoves them
into a polythene bag, locks up the office, locks the shop, and
whistles in the crisp air of another October lunch-hour.
Sometimes he really does feel alive, as when the birds hop reassuringly towards him to receive their scraps of park-bench
leftovers. At times like that he forgets that he is dirty, smutty,
lewd. He feels just the same as everyone around him. They
too, after all, have their secret lives and tentative lusts. They
are the people who would respond to a telephone number in
a newspaper, safe in their anonymity, but would not deign to
leave their name and address. They were despicable in their
anonymity. At least he was open about his work. He had
even told his mother once, discreetly, over the phone. She had
not appeared to understand, and he had left it at that. All she
seemed able to comprehend was that he was involved in film
and TV distribution. Had he met any of the actors? No,
mother, he had not. Not would wish to.

A crisp October day, as stated, it was when the nun
dropped from the sky and landed at his very feet on a quiet
path on his way home.

'In the name of Christ!' he shouted, startled. The nun was
startled also.

She looked at him for a second, her mouth open, before
turning on her heels and trotting off along the pavement. He
wiped his hand across his forehead, examining the high wall

which ran the length of the pavement. She had jumped from this wall, behind which lay the convent of the Sisters of the Sacred Heart, its glazed and bolted wooden doors standing thirty yards further up the street. He looked again at the top of the wall. It took guts to jump from a wall that high. Then it struck him: she had nearly killed him. Had she landed on top of him, had he decided a moment earlier to sprint home, he would have been flattened beneath her billowing robes. He tingled at the thought and looked along the pavement to where the nun was disappearing around the far corner. His mind made up, he began his sprint.

It took him all of a minute to catch up with her, and even then he could not bring himself to use a hand or an arm to halt her, for he was not sure whether nuns were allowed to be touched and he thought that probably they weren't. So he walked along beside the nun, trying to catch her eye, while she pointedly ignored him and walked quickly along the crackling paving stones.

'Miss, eh, Sister. Hold on there a minute. You nearly killed me back there. Nearly gave me a heart attack you did. Hold on.'

She stopped and drew breath. Her cheeks were strawberry coloured, not all with the effort of running, and her eyes were brown like a young animal's.

'Sorry,' she said. She began to walk on. He caught her up again.

'It isn't every day I encounter nuns falling from the skies, you know. What's it all about?'

'Swimming,' she said, not stopping, not looking at him.

'Swimming?'

'Though I can't for the life of me think why I'm telling you.'

'Swimming?'

'It's got nothing to do with you really. Nothing at all. Now if you'll excuse me,' and with that she began to cross the road.

'Swimming?' he called from where he stood.

She stopped in the middle of the deserted street.

'Swimming,' she said. 'Swimming, yes, swimming, swimming, swimming.'

'Alright,' he said, approaching her and wondering what she looked like beneath the thick material of her habit, 'keep your hair on. What colour *is* your hair, as a matter of interest, professional interest you understand?'

She turned away and began to walk. He walked beside her.
'Professional interest?' she said at last.
'I'm a toupee maker,' he said.
'I don't believe that.'
'And how do you expect me to believe that swimming
has anything to do with leaping commando-style from a
ruddy great wall?'
'I am about to go swimming. It is my weakness, may the
Lord forgive me. I come out of the convent twice a month
and go swimming.'
'At the local baths?'
She did not answer.
'You like swimming?'
'It is the only thing I miss, living in the convent.'
'How long have you been inside?'
'You make it sound like a prison.'
'Isn't it?'
'Certainly not. It is the very opposite. It is a liberating ex-
perience.'
He nodded, agreeably, he hoped, and she saw him nodding
and smiled just a fraction.
'You're pretty when you smile.'
She stopped smiling.
'Where's your swimming costume then?'
'At a friend's.'
'That's where you're off to just now is it?'
'Go away.'
'Okay. Goodbye, Sister.' And with that he went, but not
far. He walked around the corner and waited a minute. He
heard her shoes clack on the cobbles, then stop, checking
that he was not following, then start to move again at a brisk
pace. At that, he put his head around the corner. She was at
the end of the short street, turning into the doorway of one
of the tenements. Her friend's house, he presumed, thinking
himself clever.

That afternoon, back at the office and dealing with any
orders that came through, he toyed with his pencil and
thought of the lucky nun. She was lucky because she had her
secret life, her little thrill (there was no other, more modest
way of putting it). Perhaps technically she was sinning by
leaving her convent, perhaps she would burn in Hell for it, because she believed in Hell. She had been tempted by the
thought of a public baths, and she had fallen. She was lucky.

Life still held for her the fortnightly promise of an unjaded, vicarious pleasure. For him there was no such hope. He slotted a cassette into the recorder, turned on the television, and fast-forwarded through another romp. It was all over in less than nine minutes. He felt numb, his eyes glazed like the rainwater on that cobbled street. He thought of his nun and her swimming.

He counted out the days as if he were a child again and this his Advent. After much thought, on the ordained day he took the afternoon off and went to the baths. Not to swim, no, for his body was a mockery to him; just to watch. He paid his money and climbed the dull stairway to the spectator's gallery. A woman was up there, waving down to her children who splashed and did brave manoeuvres in order to impress her. He sat close to this woman at the very front of the balcony. And looked down. Mostly children. They screeched, and their screeches bounced off the steamy glass roof, echoing around the pool. They played and got water in their eyes and cried.
As he had once cried.
There were a couple of teenage boys as well, who walked around the edge of the pool and studied a clutch of teenage girls, three of them, who were bobbing in a ring in the centre of the water. He studied these girls, watched as one of them kicked away from her friends and swam, her legs snapping like crocodile-grips, to the edge of the pool. She eased herself out of the water and, pulling at her costume, sat at the side of the water on the warm tiles. He watched her intently through the rising wisps of steam. Blobs of eyeliner highlighted the red rims of her eyes. She pulled the hair back from her face and kicked water at her friends. The boys hovered near her, unable to make the telling move, though the girl's friends giggled encouragingly from their retreat.
He became so entangled in this burgeoning romance that he failed to notice, for some time, the elegant underwater motion of the perfect swimmer, the body at ease in its airless environment, the head arched back, eyes wide on the approaching wall, then somersault, breath, kick and away again, a half-length before another breath was necessary.
But, as the head came up again for its gulp of salty air, he caught the face, and his gaze turned away from the antics of the girls and boys. His nun was pushing her way slowly and without apparent effort throught the water, teasing it, assuring

it of its lifeless quality. This was not the splashing and stinging water of the children, nor was it the bobbing water of the girls and their desires. It was silent water, a thing to be used, a willing pet to the cutting strokes of its mistress. And she moved as though she owned it, and had trained it well. And he watched her, holding his own breath, releasing it whenever she rose out of the ripples to breathe again. He wondered what she was thinking. She looked as if her total concentration was focussed upon the act itself, nothing more, and he followed her as if she were a large and admired fish which stayed always just out of reach of his line. Slowly he became less tense. He sat deeper back into the hard wooden seat and enjoyed the performance. The slow motion. The playback.

After thirty or forty lengths she rested her shoulders against the wall at the deep end and bobbed a little, moving her feet and with her arms languid along the edges of the tiles. And it was then, as she cleared the water away from her face, that she saw him. She looked away, then looked back. Her eyes closed a little, and her mouth opened as if to suck in liquid through a straw. She gazed down on the surface of the water, which reflected his distorted image, stretching him out as on a rack. Then she kicked towards the steps and left the pool quickly.

He watched her as she glided on tiptoe towards and into the changing area. From his position he could see a tiny portion of the interior. Little girls scampered about on their toes, splashing the dregs of water around them. But his nun stayed invisible, as though she had slipped behind a mirror.

When she left the baths, not without apprehension, she was dressed in a simple frock and belted coat, a carrier-bag slung over one arm, but when she left her friend's flat twenty minutes later, she was dressed in her habit, and her whole gait had changed perceptibly: her arms now angled from the elbows, rather than retaining the straight, flowing motion they had had when she had left the baths, and her feet were placed flat on the pavement, their purpose unshakeable. He followed her all the way back to the convent, intrigued by everything, and watched as she tapped on a small side door and was allowed inside, doubtless by another willing accomplice.

He waited out his two weeks and returned to the poolside, dressed in his swimming-trunks this time and looking pale and unathletic beside the children. He blushed when some water stung him in the eyes, kicked up by an angelic monster who smiled up at her mother in the watchful gallery. He waded into the surprisingly cold water (surprising for the amount of steam rising from it) and did his imitation of a doggie paddle. After half a length he grew tired, his lungs pushing outward as if frantic for release from his rib-cage, and he half-walked to the side of the pool, resting, gripping the edge with his fingers, blowing hard. Gooseflesh settled on him, and he dipped often beneath the water. After thirty minutes of this he knew that he had scared her away. The girls were there, and their boyfriends, grappling with one another in the water until the attendant blew his whistle and signalled for them to keep their distance. Quite right, and in a public baths too. He climbed heavily out of the water and trotted to his cubicle.

A fortnight after that he went again, as a spectator this time. There was no sign of her. He reasoned that she had changed her day for coming. For a solid week of afternoons he sat it out, the woman at the kiosk frowning suspiciously at him. She knew his sort, and he knew it was useless to reason with her. When she asked him one final day what his game was, he stopped going to the baths altogether. He gnawed at himself inwardly, arguing his need to see her again. He wanted to apologise for having spied on her, wanted to tell her how much he admired her, and how much he envied her passion for swimming. But he had spoiled all that, hadn't he? She did not allow herself to go swimming now. He had put a stop to that, to her only pleasure. He needed her forgiveness; that was the truth of it. He needed to tell her about his job, about his feelings, about the way he had been nullified by it all, by what he did and what he was forced into becoming and what he had made of himself. He needed to tell someone other than himself. He chewed his pencil, listening to a morning batch of answering-machine messages and growing sick in his heart. He grew sick as he listened to click after click, as he listened to all the anonymous callers becoming afraid and deciding in a flurry of panic to remain anonymous. Even worse in a way, he listened to those who confidently gave their name and address, awaiting the sordid merchandise. One of them even said a cheery 'Thank you' before putting down the receiver. One — one of the anonymous — was abusive. He weakened, feeling his mind and his stomach churning in unison, switched off the machine, and went for a walk.

No nuns fell from the sky, but he had an idea during his stroll amongst the children and the dogs of the local common. He returned to the office and reached into the drawer for the telephone directory. He would ask if he could leave a message for her. It did not matter that he did not know her name. He would say an old friend with whom he swam regularly had joined the Order and could he speak to her please now that he was back in this country. He found the number and, his heart beating as though he were fifteen again and arranging his first date, dialled the convent.

The phone rang once and once only. That was quick. He began to speak but was interrupted.

'Hello, this is The Sisters of the Sacred Heart. Please leave your message after the signal. God bless you.'

The electronic bleep.

He opened his mouth again. An answering machine! He listened as the machine whirred, the tape running. He licked his lips. He couldn't speak to an answering machine! It was ridiculous. He tried to formulate some message, but nothing would come. His fingers trembled. Shocked, frightened, finally numbed, he slammed down the telephone, thumping on it with his fist.

'Damn you,' he said. 'Damn you, damn you, damn you.'

But in his heart of hearts he was hoping for the reverse.

VALERIE THORNTON

TINTED NEUROSIS

It shouldn't even have been raining. Not in the middle of
summer. It had been so long since Connie had felt rain that
she defied it to affect her. Nevertheless, the toes of her pale
pink satin shoes were already stained dark, with tiny grains of
dirt clustering on them. She was on a shopping expedition for
sunglasses. Pink ones with pink graded lenses. Not the easiest
to find maybe, but she could hunt here, before her train, and
at the other end too. Surely somewhere would have them.

She trailed around in the rain without success. One last
attempt left her a little short of time for catching her train.

At the station, a boy was running the wrong way, against
the motion of the long moving walkway, gaining inches for
his effort. He irritated her sufficiently for her to stand her
ground in the middle of the narrow conveyor belt, forcing
him to precede her back to his start. Serve the silly little fool
right, she thought.

The man at the ticket hatch was not only dour. He was
insolently slow. Still she had four minutes to catch the train.
Beside her, a second queue was constantly dwindling and
being replenished. However, she was now second from the
front and there was little point shifting queue. She'd only
lose more ground.

Two other ticket positions were closed while employees
idled behind the counters. But the man in front of her was
taking far too long. The sluggish ticket seller dithered around
with papers, then walked away from the counter. Now concerned about the increasing likelihood of missing her train,
she glared angrily at the counter and the back of the man in
front of her. He was in uniform. An employee. Wasting her
time. How dare he!

The sloth returned and handed over a large quantity of
money. Not tickets. And this was a ticket office! Two sig-
natures and it was her turn. And time for her train to depart.
Controlling her rage, she asked for her ticket. In slow motion,
he selected her ticket, punched it, took her money, selected
her change and shoved ticket and change so that she had to

scrabble and claw it through to her side of the perspex barrier. She felt like throwing the lot at the misanthropic flabby jowls.

She'd missed so many trains and buses that she had resolved not to make herself look ridiculous by running for a bus or train ever again. Nevertheless, she dashed towards the ticket barrier with unseemly haste. Even as she looked at the electronic timetable, her train and its stops riffled and flickered white into black. Two lads were lounging against the barrier and a little man was standing on the platform about to put a whistle to his lips.

The lads continued their conversation while one of them, in an absent-minded leisurely fashion, clipped a 'T' out of her ticket. As she ran onto the deserted platform, the guard blew his whistle.

She stopped, turned on her heels and stormed away. A second volley of whistling was shrilling out behind her and the lads at the ticket barrier were protesting to her that the train was now waiting. For her! But she couldn't possibly abase herself. Utterly furious, she turned her heels on them too. A third whistle and her train pulled out.

Attempting to appear calm, and refraining from looking around in case anyone had witnessed her little drama, she looked up at the timetable. An hour. A whole hour to kill in this wretched place. She felt like exploding, screeching, cursing and wreaking vengeance on the sluggard in the ticket office. How dare that little man with the whistle compound her fury by undercutting the justification for it! If only he'd let the train go the first time. She knew she shouldn't have run for it.

At least she had her ticket — but it had been clipped. Surely she hadn't wasted all that money too? With exquisitely balanced rage, she walked out into the rain.

She wandered the streets, getting wet, her mouth tight, her face like flint, until she felt a little calmer. She was now thoroughly soaked and convinced her search for pink sunglasses was doomed.

As soon as she was calm enough to be rational, she realised she should return to the station. The train might even be in and she could at least get on it.

It was, and she approached the ticket barrier poised to explode in the face of any ticket inspector who dared to challenge her clipped ticket. But she passed through the ticket barrier without problems. There was half an hour to wait.

What a waste of time! She could almost have been there by now.

She sat and pretended to read. The carriage was unlit and empty. Her feet and legs were dismally wet. Then someone walked past, up the centre aisle. She half wished they would attack her, so she could have the satisfaction of retaliating. Then a couple shoved and jostled their way into the two seats opposite her. She did not deign to look up at them. Their shoes and legs were dirty and shabby, their accents vulgar. She looked up enough to see her arm through his, and hated them for being in love.

At last the train started, signalled by the same sardonic whistle as the preceding one.

They went straight into the tunnel and in the dim fluctuating light of the passing tunnel lamps, she saw the couple were kissing. She hated and envied them.

As they emerged into the light, she darted a quick look at him, avoiding his face. He was fat and dirty, but happy, and kind towards the girl. She was laughing and teasing him. Resentful, Connie refused even to look at the girl.

When the seats across the aisle from her emptied, she was tempted to move. But she didn't really want to be pointedly rude to them. Besides, her anger was, at last, subsiding. She became able to read.

Smoke drifted in from the next carriage and she wrinkled her nose in distaste. As if in response to the stimulus, the man reached into his pocket. Filled with outrage, she was ready to point out in no uncertain terms that this was a no-smoking carriage. She looked directly at him, ready for confrontation, and caught the smile for his girlfriend with her own eyes, as he handed her a huge peppermint. Abashed, she returned to her book.

She finished the book three-quarters of the way through the journey. By now she could see beyond her enveloping rage. She turned and looked out the window.

It was still raining. The window was being decorated with long diamante scratches, stabbing swiftly onto the dirty glass. The couple opposite were quiet and self-contained.

For the first time, she looked at the girl's face. One of her eyes was blank and pale, without a pupil darkening the centre. The other was brown. Both were unfocussed, shifting, unseeing.

Her arm through his took on a new meaning. Chastened, she scrutinised the girl guardedly. When she turned to speak to

her boyfriend — she had no rings on — her eyes were directed
down around his shoulder level. Connie was unsure if she was
totally blind, and she didn't want to appear rude to the boyfriend either, so she returned to the glittering patterns on the
window. She wanted them to get off first, just to confirm her
suspicions.

The girl bent down and picked up her bag. Surreptitiously
Connie watched her take out her purse. Without even pretending to look, she took out her ticket. Then she asked her
boyfriend to tell her what exactly was wrong with the stitch-
ing round the zip on her bag. She could feel something
catching but needed his eyes to understand it perfectly.

As the second last stop approached, they prepared to go.
He waited until the train had stopped completely before
taking her hand and helping her out with careful tenderness.

Beyond the blurred window, Connie could see them running, laughing, hand in hand, towards shelter from the rain.

By the time the train glided into her station, the rain had
stopped and the sun was shining weakly on a rain-varnished
world.

Connie gamely ignored her still-damp legs and feet, and
smiled a sweet thank-you at the collector who took her ticket.

BRIAN McCABE

BANANAS

They have made the colour yellow
famous for its shape.

I like the way their skins unzip
and are vital in cartoon strips
for unfooting the wild escapes
of innocent villains.

Their word is a friendly name
for madness.

They have no pips, thus
may be chewed without indignity
or teeth.

They are phallic only when
it is really expected of them.

As I buy a bunch, I think
of broad-fingered hands, glinting
machettes, impending revolutions
and of a new kind of Adam
who is making his way up the Clyde
in a very proverbial boat.

They give the sedate fruitbowl
its brazen smile.

CANAL IN WINTER

How can water go into *a coma*?
Or Exhaust-pipe with raised head be
a snake in a catatonia —
having swallowed a silencer?

Is a stick, stuck to its stickness,
like anything else I've known?
Why must I construct a resemblance
of Pram-frame and exoskeleton?

All I know is I must: try again,
with a mind that's frozen over,
to thaw each thing from its name
although it's a doomed endeavour:

through this sliver of ice, I try
to make the world new again,
as a mother and child pass by
and I hear myself named, Man.

A CHALLENGE

You're stuck in your rut, old stag.
You've been domineering the season
too long. How haggard you've grown.
I've amused you before, old pro,
with my amateur, antlering antics.
You'll get a charge out of me yet.
To be perfectly blunt, I'm hacked-off
with the sight of your proud silhouette
on the lids of all the shortbread tins.
The Monarch o' the Glen bullshit.
I've been tasting the air between us
and I know that your reek is rank.
All year I've stayed in training
for this clash of horns. Listen.
I'm not all stomp and snort.
I'm no phantom of the mountain mist
nor your image come home to haunt you.
I'm not posing for a post-card. This
is your death on the dimming horizon. This
is my jagged head that's rearing
on the ragged skyline. So:

square go.

ROLAND J. PORTCHMOUTH

AUNT DOT

I said to Edith when we got home (I mean, I felt quite
    faint), I said
What's happened to the garden! Not that she was in any
    state to talk
she was trembling that violently against the coal-house
    wall: I said
What's happened to the garden! (I mean, it was up to the
    roof!): I remember
I said, walking down that lawn this morning and saying to
    myself
That's a neat lawn — a very pleasant lawn! But I mean,
    look at it, Edith,
you couldn't get through it now with assault course equip-
    ment!
Those dwarf marigolds shouldn't be up there — not with
    the sunflowers!
Where are the sunflowers? Good gracious, Edith, they're
    up to the pear tree.
And look at the hollyhocks going up past the top bedroom
    window!
Edith, I said, we must take a firm hold of ourselves. This
    is not usual.
Dahlias do not suddenly start acting like rhododendrons.
    Nor do our pansies
scowl down at us normally from over the clothes line.

You know, Edith, I said (I mean, she was looking at me
    with a stricken
unhealthy sort of expression) I said, I bet you what you
    like, I said
it's Aunt Dot! I bet what you like Aunt Dot's been here
    again.

You know, I wasn't all that happy when I left her at her
    flat last night.
She had got her electric grinding wheel plugged in in the
    lounge
and was whirling away at it with her spade and trowel
putting an edge on them like ladies' razors. And she'd
    sharpened her garden fork
so you could sew a sequin on with it.
I just had to leave: I couldn't stand the noise. I mean, I
    called out goodbye
but what with the smoke and sparks flying everywhere
    from a
power disintegrator she'd rigged up for pulverising peat
    and manure
I doubt if she even noticed me go.

I'll bet what you like Aunt Dot's been here doing her
    good turn as usual.
What can you do, I mean, with relations who insist
on being useful!

ETHEL

Ethel was never (as far as family gossip goes)
a tidy person. When she was still a girl they decided
she should move all her belongings in the cowshed
and live there with them. But she upset the cows
with her untidy ways; and had to move indoors again.
Then they tried the garden. But nothing grew much after
     that;
and then stopped coming up altogether, preferring to stay
     out of her way.
When the family couldn't stand the sight of bare earth any
     more,
they encouraged her to live in the field behind the house;
and apart from the fact the sheep have given up going there
and every hen-partridge, frog, field mouse and hedgehog
have moved everything over into Wattery Meadow
she seems to have settled down at last.
The flowers there haven't been quite their bright selves,
     never remembering
what they were supposed to look like, or whether to come
     out now or later:
(the lady's bedstraw has been afraid to show herself at all).
But as I said, apart from yellow coltsfoot and buttercup
     being blue
and blue scabious and cornflowers a kind of pink
no-one would notice that the natural order had been inter-
     fered with.

I'm only telling you this because Ethel is my favourite aunt
and I'll have to explain one day that the old gentleman
     who's been living in our henhouse
for twenty years, comparatively free from nervous disorders,
is uncle.

PERCY

He came across the field like something blowing from
    a haystack. I made
several attempts to stop him but he was going too wild.
As he sailed past me and up into the sky, the draught sent
    me spinning.

I knew this sort of thing would have to be stopped: he was
    getting
too involved with the whole business. Beside which,
it was beginning to annoy us that he was the only one who
    could do it.

He used to say (when he was just Percy and not so much
    above everything)
that he would be up there with the gulls and cormorants
    one day,
swooping about over the sea-lanes beyond Trawlers' Buoy.

I'll have to talk to him when he gets back. It's becoming
embarrassing having to keep going down to the beach with
    people round,
meeting him with towels when he comes out of the sea.

DAISY FAMILY

Miss Jenny said Why not go
and pick daisies? So Julia went
on hands and knees across the meadow, working
like a mechanical digger till she disappeared
over the sky line; and must have worked her way
roundcountry when she came in view
from the other direction, giving no sign
of ever having looked up or
stopped what she was doing. When Miss Jenny saw her far
    off
she pulled down the brim of the big straw hat
shading her from the sun; and Julia stood up
striding to her through the long grass and dropped
half the field's output on her lap. Right, she said,
counting, There's cudweed, fleabane, nodding bur-
marigold, chamomile, coltsfoot, tansies,
groundsel (both sorts), ragwort, goatsbeard,
ox-tongue, hawkbit, catsear, ox-eye,
lettuce, dandelion, agrimony, nipplewort,
hawksbeard, hawkweed, mayweed, feverfew,
sneezewort, mugwort, yarrow, gold rod,
cornflower, chicory, butterbur, burdock,
sow-thistle, woolly thistle, spear thistle, creeping thistle,
oh, and Bellis Perennis — that's the common daisy,
'prettily perpetual'. I do wish, Miss Jenny said,
you'd get your head out of books, dear, sometimes!

THE TALL THISTLE

I said to Alfred
You shouldn't be afraid of thistles.
Little ones only make you careful what you pick
or sit by. And you can see big ones.

Do you remember, I said, the big baron in Dover Castle
with armour like a drawerful of cutlery?
He could have chopped a log up
just by falling on it.
    He stood there in the middle of the stone floor
without looking; and his axe up: and couldn't drop it.
He was as cold as a frozen chicken when you touched him;
when you pushed him nothing happened.

That's what a big thistle's like, I said
as we looked up at it towering above us against the sky
and it began to lean slowly over and I stepped back.

WILMA MURRAY

KIDS LIKE THAT

Well! Well!

Just come over to this window a minute. Now, would you just look at that. There's a bonny mess.

But. I warned her. I told her there'd be trouble if she kept leaving her car there in the playground late every night. The young buggers! My God, they've done a thorough job on it. I hope she's well insured, that's all I can say.

It's her own fault, of course. I'm maybe just the janitor around here, but, oh, I see things. I see things. She should go the rounds with my cleaners some night. Minds like cesspits, half of them. Aye, the kids, I mean. If she saw some of the things they write up on the walls about her, she'd maybe change her ideas a bit. There's some of them would fancy doing a lot more to her than just spray her car. Oh, I could tell you stories!

But they never listen to me, of course. I'm just the janitor. Not that she's the worst, mind you. She's not one of those toffee-noses. You know the kind I mean. The Ah-Mr. Robertson-all-smiles type when they want me to do something then Whoosh! and I'm bloody well invisible again. No, no. She's O.K. with me. When she wants a favour, she asks nice-like. Polite. Oh, but I speak up to her. Proper-like, of course. I told her before. It was no use getting kids like that excited and stirring them up over their lessons. No use at all. It just revs them up for no reason at all then what are they going to do? They're going to take it out on something. Or somebody. I told her.

I haven't got her education or anything, of course, but I could tell her a thing or two about kids like that. I could. I haven't been janitor here for nine years and learned nothing. Oh, no. Maybe she thinks she's got them eating out of her hand, but underneath they're all the bloody same. Just young buggers. Aye, and the lasses are as bad, believe me.

She had this fancy project going on this term, you see. The Silver Jubilee thing for the school. 1959-1984. You know the kind of thing. Well, God knows what they were

getting up to in that room up there, but I was taking a sound
projector in to her and there was Cliff Richard belting out
'Livin' Doll' from a record player. You remember that one?
Got myself a cryin' talkin' sleepin' walkin' Livin' Doll. God!
And he's still on the go. Never liked him. Well, anyway. She
explained to me she was trying to bring 1959 into focus for
the class by creating 'Teenager 1959' and getting them to
compare things then with things now. Do you call that education? The kids were as happy as Larry, mind you, taking
photographs of the school, outside interviewing folk, dressing
up in the classroom. To be fair, there was a serious side to it
as well. I remember there was a display of photographs I
helped her to put up. It was good that. Showed the town, the
way it's grown since 1959. And all done by Campbell McBain,
if you don't mind. That's Skeet, in other words. Oh, you
must know Skeet. Everybody knows Skeet.

    Aye, and that's another thing. *She* even calls him Skeet.
Teachers should have more sense than that, now, shouldn't
they? Oh, aye, she's walked right into this one, I'll tell you.

    What was I saying? Oh, yes. Skeet. Now he's a right little
bugger. You know what his particular party piece used to be?
You won't believe this. But, I tell you. It's the truth. He's a
wiry sort of kid, you know. Small for his age. Tough with it.
Well, when the cars are slowing down at the traffic lights
there, just outside the school, he used to leap off the pavement and jump on to the door handles, hang on for about
five yards or so and then jump off. No. I know. I wouldn't
have believed it either if I hadn't seen it myself. You should
have seen the faces on some of those drivers. My God! The
nerve of that young bugger! I swear it was beautiful to watch.
He was caught, of course. But what can you do with a kid
like that?

    But I was telling you about this project thing they were
doing. Oh, I told her. I told her she was asking for trouble
getting them all wound up. What's the good of it, I asked her.
She said she wanted to channel their energy into something
realistic and maybe help to bridge a generation gap at the
same time. She's a history teacher, right? Well, you tell me
what you think history is. It's wars and dates and stuff, now,
isn't it? I know it's the school's Silver Jubilee and all that,
but I can't see the good of them knowing only the last twenty
five years of history. What's happened in the last twenty five
years, anyway? There hasn't even been a decent war.

    So, she got all the kids bringing in junk from 1959. You've

no idea. Old records, newspapers, photographs, clothes even.
I was in with a heavy box one day and there was this lassie
prancing around in a petticoat, one of those great sticking
out things with the layers. The kind they still wear on Come
Dancing. You know. They were all the fashion then. The kids
were laughing at it. That was called paper nylon and it ripped
your stockings to shreds, she's saying. Then one of the kids
pipes up. Stockings? You mean suspenders and things?
Ootcha! he says. No, Stevie. Not that kind, she says. Calm as
you like. Now, I ask you, is that any way for a teacher to behave? Just asking for trouble. Oh, I told her.

Then. She got the parents to come in to see the display. I
don't know how she managed it. Well, you know what they're
like around here. It's all bingo and the pub here in the evenings. School's the last place they want to be seen. You know
what they call this school, I suppose? Aye. The reservation.
Good that. Well, she got some of them in anyway. The
mothers were fair taken with it. I suppose a lot of them were
about the same age in 1959 as their kids are now. It brought
back memories for them, I think. There was this shop model
in one corner all dressed up in 1959 fashion. God knows
where it came from and I wouldn't like to ask. I carried it upstairs as well, you realise. There's some funny jobs here. Well,
the kids had put old price tags on all the clothes and I heard
one mother say to another, Look at this Jean. £2. 19. 11d
for a summer frock! And she says, That's my frock. And the
first one says, Aye. Horrible, isn't it.

The fathers now. There weren't many of them, of course.
They seemed more taken up with the teacher, though I saw a
few of them give the male model outfit a bit of a sideways
look. My God! I heard one say, we never had things like that,
did we? No, his mate says, and our teachers never had things
like that, either. I tell you. They're as bad as the bairns. They
are.

I suppose it's amazing, really, when you come to think of
it. A skinny little thing like her handling kids like that. You
can never tell by the look of them, you know. That's one
thing I've learned. There was a maths teacher here, a few years
back. Big lad. Rugby type. Well, I found him greetin' in the
boiler room. More than once. So, you see, you never can tell.

Still. Look what it's got her. I did try to warn her. You
can't say I didn't. But, Christ, that's some mess of a car.

Can you read what it says, anyway? Where's my specs?
That pink word on the bonnet, there. H, something. Oh my

God!

Well, she's been asking for it.

Oh, but hell, I can't have the lass driving into a garage with that on her car. The young buggers. Where's that spray paint I confiscated? Red? That'll do. That'll cover it.

Aye, and that's another thing. Have you noticed? The kids nowadays can't even spell.

MOIRA BURGESS

SURROGATE

'There's someone,' the old woman said, 'who knows exactly what I do and when I do it.'
I was surprised at the way she burst out with it, since of course she didn't know me at all. The two young pregnant mothers ahead of us, with whom we'd been idly discussing the headlines, had just been called, one to each surgery. Now we were alone in the waiting-room; I suppose I was reassuringly on her side of forty, and perhaps even had a good-listener look. She was quite agitated, her shiny knotted hands with the dark liver-spots folding and refolding the tabloid in her lap. 'Cathie, 83, Mugged', the blaring letters spelled.
'What do you mean?' I said, looking concerned. I was really rather interested to hear what she'd say.
For such an old bag of bones she was concise enough. 'There are notes,' she said, 'messages. Always when I'm out. The police won't do anything. They just say it must have been a friend. I tell them there isn't anybody left who would be calling, but I think they think I'm a bit forgetful. I'm seventy-nine, you see.'
'Oh, that's no age,' I said with a smile. 'My mother's over eighty and everybody says she's good for her century.'
'That's nice,' said Miss Jenner in an abstracted way. (I pulled myself up for even thinking of her as Miss Jenner. It wouldn't do if I used her name, when she hadn't given it to me.) 'They're not rude or anything, you know.'
'The police?'
'The notes,' she said a little testily. 'They say, oh, things like *Sorry I missed you*. Or *Will call back*. That worried me for a whole week. And once, *Hope you enjoyed the concert*.'
Her faded eyes held mine as if anyone ought to see the horror of that. I put on a puzzled look.
'I'd *been* at a concert,' she whined. 'Don't you see? How did they know?'
'You must have mentioned it,' I said, 'in a shop, or — or at the bus stop or something.'
'But that means they were standing near me.' Her old

hands weren't at all steady. 'Listening ... I'm almost afraid
to open my mouth now.'

You don't say, I thought sarcastically. I said in my mother-
soothing voice, 'I wouldn't worry. I'm sure there's nothing in
it. You don't get phone-calls, do you?'

'Yes!' she cried, certainly shaking now. 'They never speak.
I answer, and the phone goes down. It's got so that I tremble
for an hour. I'd have the phone taken out, but I really need it.
I have angina, you know.'

'So has my mother,' I said. 'It's a very crippling condition,
isn't it?'

'Well, it needn't be,' said Miss Jenner with unexpected
spirit. 'If you take your pills and behave sensibly, that is.'

'My mother's must be very bad. She can hardly do anything for herself.'

'Are you sure it's angina?'

'No,' I said, 'but she is.' That had slipped out: there was
an unwelcome dawning in her pale-blue eyes. Time to tip the
balance a little. 'What I would wonder about those phone-
calls, if I were you,' I said, frowning, 'is how the person
knows your number.'

'I wonder that too,' she gasped. I thought she was in for
an attack right there in the waiting-room. 'I've wondered and
wondered — '

'Perhaps a tradesman you've had in?' But apparently she
hadn't had even a plumber for years. I could imagine her
basement flat, damp-furred wallpaper, crumbling sills. 'The
meter-reader? The minister?'

'*The minister?*' That really gave her something to think
about: I was afraid I had gone a little too far. But she was a
loyal Presbyterian. 'No, no. But my name's on my pension
book ... And I suppose the chemist knows it ... And
there's the voter's roll, they could look up the phone-book
from that — '

'You might have been carrying a case with a label on it,' I
suggested, 'when you were going on holiday some time.'

That rang a bell. 'Last summer,' she said. 'I'd been ill, and
I went to a little convalescent home on the coast. Yes, I remember, I did put a label on my bag. In case it went astray,
you know.' She gazed at me, blaming herself, her fingers
splayed on her thin old chest. You could almost see the
palpitations. 'They must have been on the train! Beside me!'

'Or in the bus shelter,' I said innocently, which of course
was how it had been.

Fortunately just then the pregnant ladies emerged almost together from the two surgeries, and in a moment the two doctors' lights blinked on.

'I see Dr Fraser,' I said, getting up. 'Look after yourself now, Miss — ?'

'Miss Jenner, Emma Jenner,' said the old idiot, now in such a state that she really didn't know she was telling me.

'Emma,' I said, smiling, 'what a pretty name. My mother's name is Emily, strangely enough.'

I was in the surgery with the door closed before she had tottered half-way across the floor. Her doctor would get an earful today. I settled myself for a chat with Dr Fraser, but I'm sorry to say I didn't get the attention I deserved.

'You're in very good shape for your age, Marina.' Dr Fraser had known me from babyhood and irritatingly still used my flowery and dated first name. When mother died and I moved into a flat of my own, I would call myself Jane. 'What you're describing are tension signs. Do you get enough exercise?'

'I take Mother for her walk in the park every day.'

'How do you sleep?'

'All right, I suppose.' Except that I was constantly in a half-doze in case Mother should call. Just twice in twenty years she had called when I was too sound asleep to hear. 'Marina would sleep through the last trump,' she sweetly informed every friend who came to tea.

Dr Fraser leaned back in his chair and took off his glasses. 'How is your mother?' he said.

'She doesn't seem to keep very well.'

'She hasn't been in to see me, has she? Do you want to make an appointment for her?'

'I don't think she could get to the surgery, doctor.'

'Marina, you pass by here on your way to the park.'

I came out with that argument unresolved and a prescription for more tranquillisers. I thought I could hear Miss Jenner's breathy little voice from the second surgery. Worth hanging about in the chemist's, you never knew what you might learn; and sure enough she came fluttering along in a few minutes with a prescription in her tiny claw. We laughed and exclaimed at meeting up again so soon.

'More pills,' she apologised.

'Mine shouldn't be long.' It would be nearly as long as hers, since I'd handed it over the counter as I saw her cross the road from the doctor's. 'I'm just looking for a hot-water

bottle while I wait.'
 Choosing that, and belatedly remembering toothpaste,
kept me in the shop until Miss Jenner was stowing her bottle
of pills in her handbag. We came out together into the windy,
fresh spring day. Long ago at university I had joined the hill-
walking club. I had stood on the tops three or four times,
seeing the quilted mountains stretch north and west. Then
Mother had found out, and the idea of me in such danger had
brought on her first heart-attack. Today I wouldn't stand on
a hilltop in the cold sweet breeze. I would go home to our
too-big, musty house, and Mother would complain that I'd
been away a long time.
 'Which way do you go, Miss Jenner?'
 'Up to Thornhill, dear. It's not far away, only I have to
take it slowly nowadays.'
 'I'm just over the hill. Do let me carry your shopping-bag.'
 'That's really kind of you, dear.'
 We toiled up the hill. 'Marina, is that you? You've been
nearly an hour! Where have you been?' Miss Jenner's patient
bent head bobbed away below my shoulder, blue felt hat,
neatly rolled white hair. 'I don't think you realise, Marina,
what it's like for me sitting here alone. What if the phone
should ring? What if somebody tried the door?' My flat,
when she died, would be on the crest of a hill, fronting the
westerly breeze. 'Please shut that window, Marina. You know
about my back.'
 Miss Jenner, panting, asked humbly if she might stop for
a rest. 'You seemed to be walking a little more quickly there,
dear.' I stopped. The fresh breeze fell calm. I stood in the
dull heavy street with an old woman, as always, by my side.
 'Here we are, dear.'
 There wasn't a soul to be seen in the peeling terrace of
bedsitter houses. The other side of the street was a run-down
play-park with dogs' dirt trampled into the shabby grass. I
carried her shopping-bag down the basement steps and stood
like a dutiful daughter while her uncertain fingers turned
three keys. I leaned forward to put the bag inside the door.
There were four more steps, rather steep, leading down into
the greasy little kitchen with its old green gas cooker and its
stone sink.
 'Thank you so much, dear,' said Miss Jenner, setting her
shaky foot on the top step. 'Perhaps I'll see you again.'
 'Perhaps,' I said.
 It only took one push, and as her head struck the corner

of the sink there was one hard thud. People would take it for the slamming of a car door. 'Goodbye now,' I cheerfully said. I closed the door firmly so that the lock clicked, and went back home to Mother.

MAUREEN MACNAUGHTAN

THE ROYAL CHUTE

(A Glaswegian Fable)

We used to take turns
Sitting on a slimy wall
Watching for a hand
In a trickle of dark water.
The rats were big then
Even in the torch-light.

The Royal fed the stream
With soft, bloodless stumps.
Our enemies could swim
And hide in secret drains.
We threw bricks
At bone-crunching shadows.

Numbers were always suspect.
To play the Pied Piper
You needed a witness.
One boy carried a stick
Which he faithfully notched
With every proven claim.

I can remember drifting
Through a chilling nightmare.
My door was wide open and
The chute kept performing.
The rats were gnawing
On a mountain of flesh.

Kids inherit dangerous myths
That spread like a Cancer.
When Alec broke his arm
He suffered in silence
By the time they knew
It was out of shape.

EXPOSURE

I have dug up a worm
A great, blind, ignorant force
That slowly returned to the earth.
My spade revealed this amorous
Creature and as it slipped back I
Wondered, what divine Jupiter decreed
That all things born underground
Deserve a second chance.
It might have died with violence
Massacred by one cold thrust.

The music has suddenly stopped
The Newsman sounds concerned.
Fresh talks have broken down
The mighty powers are entrenched
Their position can change our planet.
Now I know how it feels
To try and hide yourself
In a slice of metal soil.
This garden is a battleground
But the grass won't cover me.

CAMERA STANDARDS

Like pegs on a line
We wait to shake hands
The same old questions
Come bubbling out.
Preparation is everything
To a fresh politician,
His four minute visit
Has brightened our world.
They painted the bricks
The grass and the windows,
The machines were muted
He didn't have to roar.
The canteen staff served
Off white Irish linen.
We stood for a picture
That hangs in the board-room.
It's a grand little group
The faces are radiant
You could almost believe
Except for the eyes.

RODERICK HART

STILL LIFE

The large expanse of ground outside the school
could have been a garden, but for the head.
On purely academic grounds, he fully approved
of any seed apart, of course, from that of doubt,
which took root, grew, and bloomed,
but what with the herds of wildebeeste
and the annual maintenance costs . . .
which left him with what he wanted;
gravelled ground, taking nothing away
from the building itself, the college:
good solid masonry built to last,
the present tense with the virtue of the past.

Janitors then were educated men.
Ask them to erect a Graeco-Roman theatre
of benches ranged in rows, banked in tiers —
don't try telling them what to do, they knew;
broadly conforming to a parabolic curve —
left to them, they plotted that one too.
And so the wildebeeste reached the stage
of clambering on in classes, to appear
once a year, in ascending order of age;
the wealth of the world, its entire population,
under a suitably uniform summer sky,
a visual choir, a graduated harmony of the eye.

The sun smiled on us all. But the authorities observed
with especially warm relief that, even assembled,
the common herd could not raise a common voice.
On these occasions we were led, not by a conductor,
nor yet by the head, but by the school photographer;
a methodical, grey-haired man, a photographic fate,
who wrote our doom under ritual black and negated
us all in consecutive, over-lapping, large-frame plate.
'Smile for the camera, don't be shy' he'd shout, awaiting
the last unfunny face, the last unfunny tongue stuck out.
He must have wanted to but, at that time, could not
account for us all with a single shot.

I was never the funny one, the young desperado
trapped at the party pretending to have a good time;
let alone the audacious jester, the fool who lit the flame
at both ends of a composite print of the school,
the ticket-holder for the first take who ducked out fast
behind the guests to gatecrash into the last.
What did the photographer make of him:
surely he was tempted to touch him out,
to cut him down to size, to shear, to trim?
If so, he'd documented death enough to know
the policy of the gods — regarding even identical twins
with identical clothes and victorious, fate-tempting grins.

There are always a few who live by the notion
that moving targets are safe because their speed
defies the eye. One, at least, has died by it too.
Not twice as large as life but twice as lively,
the photographer left him to his fate, presenting
a double target to an already dangerous world
and not realising till it was too late
that the first to move draws hostile fire,
the first to advance gets tangled in the wire.
Inheriting, as I do, the photographic view,
projecting the photographer's line of thought,
I'm always behind the camera now, never in the shot.

Times have changed at the school.
The herd is less tractable in the mass,
and so I rely on divide and rule
to compose them class by class.
The trick can never be worked again.
The unreflecting liveliness implicit in the ruse
has given way to safety play — playing for time,
with more to gain but just as much to lose.
Hundreds of faces inhabit my head,
of anonymous men, of men long dead.
Smile for the camera, don't be shy;
put a brave face on life before you die.

ESTHER WOOLFSON

STONE PYRAMID

The heart is a device of infinite subtlety, a mechanism of ultimate usage, practical and metaphoric. Its aesthetic value, remote from its usual portrayal, full, scarlet and symmetrical, is limited, except for those people in whose eyes the perfect machine, operating perfectly, is an object of beauty. It is an agglomeration of pulsating, mucilaginous vessels and tubes twisting upon themselves, an arrangement of valves, muscles and arteries of careful, contained obsolescence. It is designed for a certain working life and except in unusual circumstances, depending on the owner's living in a distant area of the Caucasus, lasts that long and not much more, given, of course, certain variable though at present unknown, factors.

You can't but be aware of it, lying at night with the thing beating like it does, against the sheets. It's hot at night and I throw off the covers sometimes so that I can sleep, or I turn the pillows and seek out the cool places with my cheek, and thrust my feet down to the corners of the bed where the white cotton is still smooth and cold. They can't keep the building cool and the nurses complain about the stiffness of their uniforms.

The unusual summer makes it stranger and when I forget momentarily why I'm here, I feel as if I'm on a new kind of holiday which you spend in hospital abroad. I feel so well. The grass in the park outside is bleached and light and when I was allowed to go out for my walk the other day, I noticed that the edges of the grass nearest the stone paths are burning. The leaves of the cherry trees rustle hotly in the faint breeze and the impatience we all feel, day by day as the sun rises repetitively strongly, makes us apologise routinely after our daily, hourly complaints.

'It's just that we're not used to it,' we all say to one another.

When we talked about my coming here, Andrew, who is

my doctor and my friend, and I, we discussed it in a slight,
rueful way. The light from the bay shines into the window
of his consulting room. I remember when he first bought
that house, thirty years ago, his excitement and delight in
possession, the bowl of paper-thin narcissi I carried up the
neglected driveway to Megan who was in the kitchen reading
a yellowing newspaper she'd found lining a cupboard. She
was sitting at the wooden table, just outside the shaft of
dusty sunlight which splashed a pool of brilliance into the
dim, low room. Her hands holding the newspaper, were white
to the wrists with dried clay, like a pair of cracking gloves;
her alchemist's hands which, through her sculpture, turned
base earth into something more living than gold. She looked
up as I went in.

'Someone in Glasgow murdered his wife the day Ritchie,
my brother, was born,' she said.

The tide brought the glint of reflected light into the room
and away again as if a cloud had passed over the sun.

'We're all wearing out now,' Andrew said.

He sat still in his chair and made none of the gestures you
make to cover silences. I was angry for a moment but then I
saw that the faint greyness round his jaw which had been
there for years had spread somehow, and become endemic. I
felt as though my blood had ceased to flow altogether, and I
was cold. After a minute, the sun filled the room again and
my blood began to circulate and I warmed up quickly.

A nurse has come in and put my tea-tray down. We exchange a few words about the heat and unbidden, she picks
up the packet of biscuits from my locker and puts them on
the tray. I bought them in the Polish shop on the other side
of the park. They must have been left over from last Christmas, or bought early for next because they're the sort you
hang from the tree, stars and rocking horses and Hansel and
Gretel houses.

'Shall I arrange for you to go to Edinburgh?'

'Why not? I'd like to have some time there, if I ever get
out of hospital,' I said.

'Why shouldn't you? Coronary grafts are routine now,
like mending u-bends.'

I pointed out that the analogy was inelegant. I knew why
he'd used it though. They'd been having the lead tank in their

house changed and you can't always free your mind of assoc-
iations. Hearts are a bit like that anyway, with their flow and
their pressure and their valves. Andrew apologised and said
that at least Mr Kennedy wouldn't be doing it. No, not familiar
Mr Kennedy, somebody else entirely, somebody who sometimes could make new working hearts out of old bits and
sometimes couldn't.

'Look at Anna now.'
He had sent Anna to Edinburgh, two years ago it must
be. She was blue and gasping when she went and pink and
bright when she came back. I met her standing by the shore,
breathing in the air, sniffing the ozone like a dog. I talked to
Andrew about it just after she came back.
'Anna seems very well.'
'So she is. A complete repair — they did it beautifully.' I
didn't like the way he used the language of aesthetics to describe something so ugly. When I said so, Andrew replied,
rightly I suppose, that aesthetics aren't the sovereign territory of the retired art teacher. Sometimes though, I turn a
chicken's heart on my chopping-board with the point of a
knife and I'm revolted by its wrinkled, striated ugliness.

Anna didn't tell me anything about it when she came
back. She told me about the meals and the ward and described
how she'd nearly scalded herself in the bath one morning.
She didn't tell me how she felt before they put her to sleep
or what it was like to wake up renewed. Perhaps you can't
tell these things. I was going to visit her before I left but I
decided it was best not to. I remember what it was like waiting outside the examiner's room for a viva. You were one
with the others, one in reluctance and fear and ignorance, but
once they'd been into that room and said their bit, they were
changed by the experience. After that, you resented their en-
couragement since you alone then, knew the distance to your
own Rubicon.

The small, spiced biscuits taste good dipped in the tea.
Trolleys rattle up and down the corridor. Doors open and
close and white hats flit past the glass door panels. A nurse
escorts little Mrs Paine down to the lavatory. Her face is permanently pinched and anxious.

They sent me a card telling me the date and the time I

was to present myself here. I wrote it in my diary like the
date when the men were coming to mend the damp patch
on the wall under the window where the plaster bulges and
flakes and gives off a penetrating smell of decay.

I decided I'd like to spend a couple of nights in a hotel, a
good hotel, as a treat. I didn't want to go straight from the
train to give myself into the care of the hospital and Professor Donaldson, so I wrote off and booked myself a room. I
didn't want the journey spoiled by a sense of dread because I
love trains and something to look forward to at the other end.

It's easy to put your things in order when you live by
yourself. I sorted out most things before I left but I remembered after I had gone that I left washing in the basket in the
bathroom.

As it turned out, I didn't have a chance to think about
anything much on the train because a baby sitting with her
mother opposite me, began reaching out for me, stetching
across the table to hold my hands. She laughed and made
earnest though unintelligible noises. I held her hands and
made noises back and pointed out cows and sheep in fields
for her as we passed. Her mother asked if I was going to Edinburgh for the festival and I said yes.

Mrs Pyke and Miss Sandys walk past. They both have on
quilted nylon dressing gowns. Mrs Pyke's is pink, Miss Sandys'
white. Mrs Pyke wears high heeled mules. They look in, wave
and pass on. They're both Jehovah's Witnesses and talk about
it all the time. I heard them one night in the television room
saying to one another how absurd, that some people think
we're descended from monkeys. They laughed and shook their
heads, deeply shocked. The news was on and the tall, fair
woman with the raw, big-boned face and muscled forearms
got up and abruptly changed the channel. I came back to my
room. They all talk about who has what and whose condition
is worst and what operations they're all to have. They talk
about blockages and nerves and blood as if they were a new
style of shoes or a knitting pattern or a dangerous, dirty story.

The room is so hot in the afternoon. My bare feet on the
tile floor form a cool patch for a second before the tiles and
my skin adapt to one another and feel the same. The heat on

the balcony is terrific. People are sunbathing in the park and the tent where a dance company from South America is performing, sits on the grass, translucent and bulbous, like a blister. In the evenings, I sit on the balcony and listen to the music and watch people flooding in to see them, or strolling in the cool air. It's much easier for me now that I'm away from it, and can watch from a distance. When I was down there, too many promises were offered; I felt too involved.

I feel well, I breathe freely. I wonder why they are doing this to me. When I was at the hotel, I found if I did everything carefully and slowly, I had almost no pain at all. Today is Wednesday. Here, Wednesday is distinguished for one thing. It is the day Professor Donaldson does his ward round.

In the tent, a young man eats fire and a girl dances atop a pyramid of stones.

There are soggy bits of biscuit at the bottom of the teacup.
'Yuk,' the nurse says, 'how could you?'

When they took my luggage up to my room in the hotel, I gave the boy his tip and then closed the door triumphantly. I jumped on the bed and danced a bit in the middle of the floor. My things looked lost on the vast marble surfaces in the bathroom. All my bottles and jars and soaps should have been at least three times the size they were to match up. I looked in the mirrors which reflected me again and again. I was bright eyed and only a little blue round the mouth.

They gave me a pass to show I was staying there, otherwise I wouldn't have got back in after being out at night. They had to do that because it got so busy with people wanting to sit in the bar between shows.

They operate here on a Friday. They've finished all the preliminaries now, my blood is cross-matched, my E.C.G.s done. I've got a book with me that I've always wanted to read and I don't know whether to start it or not. I've been putting off reading it so that I would have something to look forward to but now, I don't know what to do. I've left too little time for it. I know it sounds funny but I couldn't bear just to read half of it. I don't know what's going on because

I haven't bought a newspaper. The world outside seems distant and irrelevant. I hate the television room which is always
filled with a pungent mixture of cigarette smoke and macabre
gossip.

This morning when I was standing on the balcony, I saw
the dancers preparing the tent for this evening's performance.
They left the tent flaps open, I suppose to let some air in. I
could see a small, dark man painstakingly building up the pile
of stones, putting one neatly on top of the other until it
looked like a cairn I found once when I was walking on
Buachaille Etive Mòr. Someone had piled up the rocks carefully so that the sides of the cairn were quite smooth and
close. I moved the top stone of the pile away and looked
down to the eyeless sockets of a sheep's skull which someone
had picked up on the hill and put there.

One night, I stayed out really late. I went to the theatre
and for a meal, and then walked very slowly back to the hotel.
Everyone is transformed by the heat. This summer has worked
on them, changing them so that now, they're open and bright
and optimistic. Just walking through the streets, I passed
churches and halls and basements, all of them turned into
theatres, and from every one, the sound of applause, or de-
clamation or laughter floated on the still, heavy air. When I
got back, there was a throng of people outside the hotel,
trying to get in. Some of them were wearing the kind of
masks they wear at the Venice carnival, sequinned, or with
cruel hook noses which gave the wearers the faces of medieval
mountebanks. The women had on brilliant, elaborate dresses.
They were remonstrating with the hall-porter who stood in
front of the doors which whirled emptily behind him. For a
moment, they seemed threatening and anonymous and then
they decided to go elsewhere and walked off laughing and
trailing bright satin on the pavement.

This morning, the professor came on his ward round.
There were so many people with him that they crowded the
room. Sister was bright pink and looked as though she had
been autoclaved. Something silly and coquettish in her
manner towards him made me think that she would shortly
take his arm and whirl away with him to the music of the or-
chestra which would strike up. He was quiet and polite and
restrainedly reassuring. (Sister may well waltz down the ward

with him, or tango in the corridor, but our relationship is
one of the heart.) He looked at me over his half-glasses. Aha,
so he's wearing out too.

The show in the tent will be starting soon. It gets quite a
bit cooler in the evening and I take my chair out onto the
balcony to listen to the music. One evening, after the performance was finished, I saw the dancers coming out and
crossing the park to go into town. As they passed along the
path under my window, they looked up and I waved down to
them. They all waved back and called greetings to me. I expect someone has told them that this is a hospital. I feel
proprietorial now and I'm always pleased when I see that
people are queuing for tickets.

At night, I sleep and wake and dream, without knowing
which is which. I dreamed about the cairn, walking, finding
the stones and in my dream, the dancing girl fell from it and
was hurt so that they brought her here. (It must have been a
dream, there is no rationality in dreams which would explain
why she was brought to a cardio-thoracic unit.) The nurses
put her in the unoccupied bed in my room and after they had
left her, I stealthily got out of bed in the twilight and went to
look at her and when I got close to the bed, there was nothing
there, only a faint scattering of grit or sand on the white cover.

Thursday tomorrow. The trolleys for supper have started
clanging in the corridor and the smell of boiling potatoes
creeps in under the door.

This afternoon, there was a card from Megan. 'A card for
you dear,' the nurse said and stayed with me while I opened
it. I showed her the picture. She was clearly disappointed and
I could see her thinking how unsuitable it was. She said it was
very unusual. It was a sketch of one of Megan's sculptures, of
a thin, naked woman, stretching upwards. I propped it against
the water carafe.

The nurse takes my supper tray away and castigates me
for not eating. I apologise and say it's because of the heat.
Tomorrow night, they'll have to start starving me, so I might
as well begin now.
'You've got to keep your strength up,' the nurse says.

The music is playing in the tent. It beats and wails and serenades me here on my balcony. It's exciting strange music, wild and wonderful and moving. People seem exhausted by it and come out quiet and bemused.

When we were at art school together, I used to pose for Megan. She's always liked thin people as models. I used to grow cold squatting on the floor, or sitting blankly in a chair while she hummed tunelessly, the tip of her tongue protruding slightly from between her lips and curling upwards towards her nose. I knew she was very talented but I didn't realise how much until one day, she let me drop my pose to see the small working model she'd made. It was so like myself, thin and broad, alive with a muted, desperate vitality, that I felt drained, as if she'd taken my strength and poured it, through her hands, into my likeness. I still remember that atavistic knowledge and the feeling of power draining and failing as I stood there naked. We were both elated.

They will open my sternum from neck to waist and attach me to a bypass machine which will do the work of my heart and keep me alive while they repair my coronary artery. They will remove a piece of vein from my leg and with it, re-place the section of artery which no longer works.

Tomorrow evening, I'll write back to Megan. I'm keeping the time specially. I'll tell her about the professor and about sister and Mrs Pyke and Miss Sandys and their singular con-versation. I'll tell her about the dancers who waved to me and about the girl and the stone pyramid. I shall tell her how I can imagine everything in her garden wilting and I'll tell her that here, the grass is burning. I must remember to tell her about the washing in the bathroom basket.

Tonight, my heart will beat against the sheets, as it does. If I lift my arm above my head as I lie, my ribs are flat against the bed and the rhythmic beat feels mystically powerful. To-night, it will beat against the sheet and tomorrow it will do the same, but probably faster. When they come to offer me sleeping tablets, which they do every night, I'll refuse them as I do every night. I want to hear people talking in the park down below and the sound of the single owl hooting and a motor bike on the main road and later the song of the drunk man stumbling across the grass. And Friday night?

Tomorrow evening, I'll write . . .

Oh Megan who can cast bronze into limbs, form marble into flesh, make me a new heart.

DEBORAH MOFFATT

FOR A JUST CAUSE

When the tour ended, abruptly, Gordon remembered the woman in Belfast. He had never really forgotten her but he had tried not to think about her. Somehow her words kept buzzing in his ear like a chorus in all his songs.

He hadn't understood her at first and her words only filled his mind with nonsense like a 'fol-de-diddle-da' refrain. But now through the anaethesia and what was probably the pain the words had a cutting edge so sharp and clear that there was no mistaking their purpose. Her voice, soft but precise in its soft Ulster inflection, supplanted his own voice, was the only voice he could hear at all inside his mind.

They had played Belfast near the beginning of the tour. The show had gone down well, with the house nearly full and the audience reasonably lively though it seemed to Gordon that he had pleased the audience less than the local fellow who opened the show, a singer who was very amusing. Gordon was not amusing. He was serious. He didn't need laughs to get his audience going. He did get the crowd singing and clapping with old songs like 'Angola' or 'Song for Che'. But some of his best material was about Ireland and the promoters had asked him not to sing any 'dangerous' songs. He had agreed against his better judgement and knew as the concert was ending that he had made the wrong decision. He wanted to sing dangerous songs. He wanted to provoke a reaction, even a dangerous reaction, from this quiet, complacent Belfast crowd. But it was too late. The program was set and he was afraid to change it at the last minute.

After the show he went to a pub with a handful of fans from the audience, his musicians and the singer who opened the show. Everybody knew each other but he knew nobody. They all talked about music, other music, not Gordon's songs. They weren't really his fans, he knew, these folk musicians who sat around playing reels and jigs for hours. They went along to his shows because they agreed with his message but thought more about their own music than his message.

Gordon knew who his fans were. He had one set of fans

among older people, people who had listened to him all along,
from the time he first came to Britain singing the songs of
Dylan, Tom Paxton, Phil Ochs. Recently he had gained a new
set of fans, young kids who filled out his concerts with bright
colours and loud noise, screaming out the words of his songs
and chanting slogans. Their presence was pleasing and encour-
aging — he was glad these kids cared about the things he was
saying. At least, they seemed to care. They made enough
noise. But there was something odd about them, alien and in-
human. They dressed in a uniform of tatty black clothes and
multi-coloured scarves, unisex haircuts and make-up. Even
their expression was uniform, with a sullen set to the mouth
and a vacant, defensive cast to the eye. He sometimes wondered if they really understood his songs. He wanted to inter-
rupt his concerts to speak to them, to ask them questions and
hear them answer in sentences instead of slogans.

None of these young fans had come along to the pub in
Belfast which was good because they unsettled him and after
a concert he didn't want unsettling companions. The pub was
very relaxing and quite sophisticated — the teenagers would
have been out of place there. Gordon himself felt out of
place in the nearly elegant lounge. The walls were panelled
with a smooth light wood. Glasses sparkled over the bar. The
people sparkled too, intelligent eyes gleaming out of handsome faces and bright conversation flooding the air.

Sitting beside Gordon was a woman who did not sparkle
and did not talk. Like Gordon, she was older than the others
and probably felt equally out of place. She sat with her hand
wrapped round a half-pint of Guinness and rarely drank from
the glass. She was dark-haired and dark-eyed. Her skin was
smooth and even, untouched by the harsh northern climate
or the stress of the troubles. Gordon liked her look. She was
the sort of woman he had great success with — a woman who
was just a little too old to seriously expect his attention and
was therefore grateful to receive it. As she was silent and
alone Gordon thought he should speak to her. Nobody was
trying to talk to him anyway.

'Hello there,' he said. 'Were you at the concert?'

'I went with my son,' she answered softly.

'Your son? Surely you haven't got children old enough to
take to my show.'

'My son is eighteen,' she said flatly, scorning the overly
obvious flattery.

'Well, did you like the show?' he asked, wondering if the

son had dragged the mother along or vice versa.

She shrugged. 'I knew your wife. I came to see what you were like these days.'

'Knew my wife?' He shifted uneasily on the hard chair.

'At university — ages ago.'

She did not have to point out that her university days were long gone. Gordon could see that easily. 'Of course,' he said. 'That was a long time ago. We're divorced now, I'm afraid.' He said it mournfully, dipping his face to look up at her with sad eyes.

Cathy had divorced him ten years ago. She had gone off with a civil servant, some bourgeois bastard who would bring home a steady pay-check and keep the kids happy with capitalist crap, television and new cars and holidays in France. That was what Cathy had wanted all along, apparently.

Cathy was Scottish. He had met her in Canada where he was living and she was visiting. They married there but she had insisted they live in Britain. America and Canada, she said, were sick societies, materialistic and spoiled. He agreed, of course, and came back to Britain with her, to live a spartan life under a promising welfare government that was closer to their ideals than the capitalist rat race in North America.

In Britain Cathy had jobs and Gordon sang his songs. Mostly he sang to himself but swore that someday somebody would listen. Cathy had believed in him, back then. But she couldn't stick it out, being weak and as it eventually turned out, false. He never knew, later, whether she had ever really believed in the things he stood for or whether she had just pretended all along in order to make him love her. The point was she did change or simply stopped pretending. When she left him she left behind all her socialist principles and her revolutionary commitment and instead committed herself to material goods and a man who would give them to her. Before she left she would scream at him that she couldn't take it any more, living without a car and a washing machine and a telephone, not with two kids and working all day. He didn't like living like that either but he wasn't about to sacrifice his principles for material goods; she knew that he could never go out and get a routine job just to keep them comfortable. She knew when she married him that he had a mission and would not forsake it for anything. She accused him of sacrificing his kids' welfare for his ego, not his principles. Obviously that was near the end of their marriage. She was no longer the kind of person he wanted to know, much less call

his wife.
'I still see Cathy sometimes,' he said now. 'I'll give her
your regards.'
'Don't bother. We didn't really see eye to eye.'
'Neither did we, eventually.'
'You changed?'
'No, she did.' Gordon lifted his head high. '*I* have never
changed. Never swayed an inch from my position.'
'Ah,' she said.
'She said that she wanted her kids to have a normal life.
I couldn't give her that. Not if we were going to stick to our
principles.'
The woman did not utter the sympathetic sounds he ex-
pected to hear.
He continued: 'We used to think that money didn't
matter. That's why we came back here to live, where there
was health care and other things you'd have to pay for in
America. We didn't need money. I didn't, anyway, but Cathy
did. She wanted more. All her socialist ideals went out the
window. She wanted more for the kids.'
'I can understand that,' the woman said.
'They didn't need more,' Gordon said but without much
conviction. He knew there was no point in saying more.
Women had a blind spot when it came to kids, a maternal
conviction which over-ruled rational thought. He decided not
to talk about Cathy any more.
'You yourself must have been politically active in the
days when you and Cathy were mates,' he suggested.
'A little. I don't think it was politics, exactly. We cared
about similar things.'
'Would you like another drink?' he asked, seeing that she
had finally finished her half-pint. He had finished his own
drink and had been calculating the cost of the round while
she spoke. He missed what she said but he wasn't bothered.
He was certain that any political activities she had indulged
in were long forgotten or anachronistic. He had no desire to
start talking about old battles.
The woman did not refuse his offer of a half-pint. When
he returned from the bar he pulled his chair closer to hers. He
had no choice: the crush of bodies around their table forced
them to sit together intimately. The woman pulled back but
could not move far.
'Anyway,' he said, 'I'm sure you're on my wavelength.'
He smiled at her, pleased by her appearance. He looked her

over openly, searching for breasts under the baggy sweater, noting that her legs were very thin. He liked women to be tiny, like children.

'I beg your pardon?' she said, blushing under his stare.

'You know. You must be more or less where I'm at, coming to my concert and all.'

'Where are you at?'

'One hundred per cent behind what I sing, that's where.'

'I see,' she said. 'You mean, you believe in — '

He interrupted her: 'In freedom and justice.'

'In killing.'

'Who says?'

'You do,' she pointed out, 'in your songs.'

'Fighting, sure,' he said. 'Fighting for freedom.'

'Killing for freedom.'

'If you want to put it that way.'

She looked around her, studying the people in the pub. 'You'd kill a man because he didn't agree with you?'

'I would kill a man for a just cause,' he said. He wondered if he were speaking too loudly. His accent, still unmistakably American after all these years, always seemed to stand out in a crowd. People were looking at him.

'How do you know what a just cause is?' she asked.

'It's obvious, isn't it?' he answered, careful to lower his voice.

'No, it isn't. To me nothing is obvious. I question everything.'

'Of course you do. Of course!' His voice got loud again. He nodded his head emphatically and he felt the liquor flood his brain. He was drinking whisky now along with his second pint. He loved the strong warm taste of whisky but could not control or predict its effect. 'We all question,' he said. 'Self-criticism is essential. So is reflection. And then the path becomes clear.'

'Your songs don't encourage reflection,' she said.

'No. I want my songs to influence people, to make them act. People have to get moving. They've been sitting back just thinking for too long. It's time to get up and fight.'

'My son, for example.'

'Your son what?' he asked. What a bizarre conversation! He wished he hadn't spoken to her. What the hell did her son have to do with anything? Why did women always have to get personal when they discussed political issues?

'He hears your songs, the ones that glamorize violence,

that idolize revolutionaries — '

'Glamourize! That's not exactly right, lady. I place revolutionaries in their proper historical perspective.'

'My son gets the message that the best way to fulfil himself, the best way to be a man, is to go out and fight.'

'And what's wrong with that, for christ's sake?' His second pint was nearly finished and he was bursting for a pee. He couldn't follow this woman's logic and doubted that she had any. 'What's wrong with fighting for what's right, dammit? It's better than sitting back and letting some pig government walk all over you. It's better than fighting for their dirty wars.'

'No it isn't,' she said. 'It is no better to kill for one reason than to kill for another. It only perpetuates a cycle of death. War will never end war.'

'I never said anything about ending war! I'm just talking about fighting for what's right.'

'The president of America thinks he's fighting for what's right. He believes it's right to drop a nuclear bomb to get rid of people like you.'

'Lady, you're talking oranges and I'm talking apples.'

'I'm talking survival.'

Survival! This woman wouldn't survive two days in the real world, he decided. He stood up abruptly. 'Excuse me,' he said. He thrust his way roughly through the crowd with no further excuses.

As he peed he knocked his knuckles against the wall, hard. He wanted to strike out, to prove his point with power and force. Arguing was always a frustrating exercise. He could never make people see. He had been trying to get people to understand him for twenty years! Most people just wouldn't listen. Some, like this woman, argued inanely. He sometimes thought he would rather be blind, deaf, and dumb. Then he would not see injustice, hear stupid arguments and crooked tales, or be driven to speak out.

He wished the woman would leave the pub. He wanted another pint but wanted no further conversation with her. He stood by the bar hoping that she would leave. He couldn't just drink in another part of the bar because he didn't want to lose sight of his coat, an expensive leather coat which had cost him a good portion of the advance on his record. Anybody might steal the coat.

The woman saw him standing at the bar. She stared at him. It crossed his mind that she was waiting for him to invite her to share his bed. What an idea! He moved quickly to the table and grabbed his coat brusquely, rushing to save himself from the inevitable. 'Gotta go, getting late. Nice to meet you,' he muttered. 'Listen,' she said. 'No, really, gotta go,' he insisted, moving away. She grabbed his sleeve and pulled him close to her. 'Listen,' she said. 'If you give yourself the right to kill somebody, somebody else gets the right to kill you.' She let go of his sleeve. 'Can you live like that?'

'Of course,' he snapped. 'Everybody does.'

'Yes, we do, because of people like you.'

He turned and left her, gouging his way to the door through the unyielding crowd. Once outside he shook himself to free his mind of all her muddled nonsense. He wondered if she were mad. She had looked like a witch, all dark and skinny, foretelling gloom and doom and ready, probably, to feast on the bones of all mankind. She wasn't normal, of that he was certain, but then with some charity he allowed that no person in Ulster could be entirely normal after so many years of violence.

The tour had continued: Dublin, Liverpool, Birmingham, the continent. He had done well on the continent even though nobody seemed to know the songs or care about the words. 'They just come to see us because we're foreign,' said his back-up guitarist, Jimmy. Gordon thought that was unkind and cynical.

The tour had been everything he had ever hoped for: an endless fantasy of nice hotels, bright cities, warm bars, friendly people. It was nothing like the years of travelling around from folk club to folk club, town hall to town hall, unknown and unnoticed. They even asked for several encores. His musicians sometimes referred to the diligent work of the promoters, as though to hint that the promotion itself brought the audience in, not the music. Gordon disagreed: no amount of promotion could be a substitute for the message. People came because they wanted to hear what he had to say.

Spain had been even better than France. He had a good repertoire of songs from the civil war and several songs about Latin America. He had songs about Che, about Cuba, about Nicaragua. When he sang out 'Death to the Yankee' in his song about El Salvador he could hear a roar of approval.

In Spain everything was good — the food, the wine, the women. In Barcelona he had nearly proposed to a beautiful woman. In Madrid he had got very drunk and had been carried to his bed by Jimmy. In the morning Fred, who played bass guitar and was a recruit from a rock band, said, 'How can you stand in the front ranks of the revolution if you're falling down drunk?'

'Piss off,' Gordon said.

'Bilbao tonight,' Jimmy said. 'The word is to go easy. The promoters don't want much excitement.'

'Where the hell is Bilbao?' Gordon asked. 'Why do they get special treatment?'

'Basque country,' Jimmy said. He lit a cigarette and smiled through its concealing haze. 'I thought you knew where every terrorist movement on earth was.'

'Put that damn cigarette out,' Gordon said. The musicians knew damn well they weren't supposed to smoke around him. If the smoke damaged his voice the tour would be finished. They didn't seem to care much, though, about the tour or his health or about anything at all. 'I've got a hangover as big as bloody Spain,' he said. 'That cigarette'll make me throw up.'

'You drank all the wine in bloody Spain, that's why,' Fred said.

'Basques,' Gordon said. 'You guys should support that. It's like Scotland or Wales, you know, wanting autonomy.'

'Yeah, that's cool,' Jimmy said. 'I'm going up to pack, you guys coming?'

It was no good, Gordon thought, seeking refuge in the coffee which was too black and bitter for his taste. Those guys would never learn to think. The hell with Scotland, he thought. If they don't want to be free that's their problem.

He spread butter on a piece of bread and ate it, grinding it slowly in his teeth to keep his head from aching. A Spanish breakfast was bird food, just dried bread and tasteless butter. His stomach demanded eggs and bacon and potatoes, the decent western breakfasts his mother had made on weekends at home in Oregon. He sometimes wondered why he had ever left home. Everything he wanted was there: good food, good friends, a good tavern. He even had a decent girlfriend there once. If he had married her, *she* wouldn't have run off with some bloody civil servant. But he had left home because he couldn't get along there: nobody used their minds or wanted to know what was on his. He had gone away to study but he hadn't liked the way they had tried to make his mind up for him at the university. He had dropped out of school only to find that the military had plans for him. He had run to Canada to avoid the draft. He had once been called a coward for evading, not resisting, the draft. He was no coward. The memory of that accusation still rankled. He had told the woman in Belfast that he would fight for a just cause and he meant it.

In Bilbao he did not pay attention to the promoters' request. He hadn't spent twenty years struggling to sing his songs just to be told now what not to sing. He sang every inflammatory song he had and waited for the city to ignite. But the audience was small and strangely quiet. They applauded weakly and left after one encore which they did not even request.

After the show the musicians would not go out with him. 'We've been out boozing every night for weeks,' Jimmy said. 'Anyhow I don't feel much like it. That concert was a downer. They didn't exactly want to be told to get up and fight, man.'

Gordon didn't argue. 'That's cool. But a drink is just what I need. See you guys later.'

'Watch yourself,' Jimmy said. 'It's cowboy country out there. Dangerous.'

'Hey, you know me. I thrive on the stuff.'

'Sure you do,' Jimmy said. 'Sure you do.'

Gordon walked around looking for a bar. The bars he passed on the street were full of noise and unpleasant smells, garlic and fish and frying fat. For the second time that day he wished that he were back in Oregon where at least a man knew where to find a drink when he needed one.

He hesitated in front of a poster of himself. Something was written on it in Spanish. He could pick out the word 'fascist' and also 'people' — or did 'pueblo' mean town? He wondered if the writer were praising him or damning him. Some artist, perhaps the same fellow, had seen fit to blacken his eye with a pen. He rather liked the look of himself with a black eye — he looked like the sort of man who would fight for his rights. Laughing at himself, he took a pen from his coat pocket and lifted his arm to blacken in the other eye.

He got no further. A siren sounded not far away and he froze: were they after him? Was it a crime to deface your own face in a Bilbao street? What kind of police state was this anyway? He would show them. He would stand up for his rights.

But stand up he did not. The bank across the street erupted in flames and flying shards of glass and the noise or the surprise or the shock knocked him off his feet. The Basque guerillas had struck again, fighting for what Gordon would have to agree was a just cause.

In the hospital bed he picked at the bandage on his hand and waited to be discharged. His injuries were not serious and he had gotten over the shock, mostly. All that remained to heal was his voice which no longer spoke words or even sounds without a great deal of effort. The doctors assured him that there was nothing wrong with him but trauma. Even so, they said, it was most unusual to develop laryngitis — real or imagined — after a bombing.

The tour was over. His brief success was over. The musicians had gone back to Britain. The promoters were not terribly upset since they had insured themselves against any possible disaster. Gordon of course had no insurance: he did not believe in it as a matter of principle.

In the hospital bed he worked and worked on his voice, desperate to produce a few words, but mostly he found that he had nothing to say.

ANDREW GREIG

WAITING, AT READINESS
(May 1940)

Tim, looking up from his mag., 'What d'you make of this,
      scruff?
"There are no roads into Nepal, but many roads within it." '

        (I cannot take you into this country.
        I can no more give you what's happening here
        than hand you the wind in a box.
        There's only one way into Nepal, everyone
        knows it; you slog it alone, in silence, on foot.
        Look at me when I'm speaking to you!
        And you look and look till it's finally clear there's
        no one there, just you, you and a few scraps of paper,
        prayer-wheels, ghosts if you believe, and the wind
              moving
        between the rocks and the rain, but now the rain is
              the real rain
        and the wind is the certain wind, and your feet
              are standing
        where all roads begin . . .)

'I wouldn't go there in a hurry.'
'No,' says Tim, 'no one does.'

Wind through our hair, feet on parachute packs, sun in
      the eyes
and clouds gathering, mountainous English clouds, waiting
      at readiness
beyond easy saying.

(From *Rumours of Guns*)

AUGUST 1940

'Finest summer I remember' Old George said
without irony, straightening his hollyhocks.
Right enough, old son, the sun day after day
and nowhere to hide in the sky, men charred
to wavering black sticks against the glare.
Fruit drop with soft thuds through the night
and lie nestling bruises in the grass
like the lovers who giggle it seems
from every hedgerow in England.
Wasps crawled from the plum she picked
but were too groggy to fly or sting
and I felt drugged with heavy juice as I
leaned to flick them from her arm ...

'Keep out of mischief, young feller' Old George said
and giggled as he shuffled off, leaving me
with fingers clenched around a windfall Cox's
still fizzling along the edges of my last bite —
I sling it away and hurry to meet her
before heat goes out of the day.

(From *Rumours of Guns*)

NORMAN KREITMAN

READING A MAP

In the centre here it is obvious
that one thing leads to another.
But there, at the edge, the land
becomes a strip of white. Some say
that is the country for growing old
where each morning you open the shutters
on landscape carefully rearranged
since yesterday to match your dying.
Distance depends upon your memories.

Others deride these tales, assert
that in the bland and rolling margins
cheerful agnostics dwell, such
as will not fix a river's course
not tolerate hills in permanent station.
They nod and smile, and pleasantly
agree with the breeze, admire the clouds.
Wine set at their table turns
instantly to water. They never speak,

The truth along that line is easier;
the world simply ends. This you may confirm
any night as you lie in bed:
just stare at the ceiling, think
how rectangular is your domain.
For you too may stretch your legs,
sideways are lord of several inches
and round about in the waiting dark
your hand may verify the edge of nothing.

ORDERS TO THE DEPUTY MINISTER

Explain to the ambassadors about the giants.
Discourse on how so long ago
they planned our city, squared the public roads,
set up the forum, the bingo-halls, the parks.

Those puissant ancestors, whose names we bear,
establish the virtue of our line
for they are certain fact, or so the legend
undoubtedly asserts (what legend?).

Next, mention the prophets who when drunk
precisely foretold the coming of the gods
who brought us compass and radar,
knots to bind us, language and skill to lie.

All this our archaeologists attest, and science
only affirms what every true man knows,
or hopes was so, or perhaps might only
take as his possibility. So with the second gods

and thence down their generations, the story
enriched with alternatives like a branching river
as heavenly cohorts descended in waves.
A pity no-one living could recognise them now.

And if the ambassadors should say 'So,
all is supposition, fables by a hidden voice'
reply to them in tones of great severity
'No. Undoubtedly we are as we were made.'

Explain to those rude envoys that any man
who as a friend would travel towards us
must come by the old road, his passport
graced by the broken giants and every derelict god.

PAT GERBER

SHADOWS FALL

The sound of the kettle strains into the silence. A floorboard creaks under my pink-slippered foot. I go through the comforting routine of tea-brewing; real leaves, none of your old bags for me. Especially not on a morning like this, after a night like that.

In the dark hall behind me chimes the grandmother clock, brassily announcing 5 a.m. And he's still up there. What ought I to do? Something, surely, if I'm a mother worth the name.

All night I'd lain awake thinking of Marie my daughter. I'd tried to visualise what my mother would have done in similar circumstances. I failed. The situation simply could not have arisen.

Things had been different then. And in some ways worse. There had been a curfew operating in our house when I was seventeen. Home at nine most nights. My young men had seen me home, given me an inexpert peck in a doorway long before we got there, and left the minute my father opened the front door. I had learned, painfully, that my father had to be obeyed. With apparent docility I evolved a way of surviving his rules. So strong was the call of young life being lived out there in the real world, I often listened for his snores, then shinned down a well-placed drainpipe to rejoin whatever party was going on. Johnny and I had slept rough under the trees. Then I'd clamber back up the pipe in the small hours, certain that my father would hear my very heartbeats. He never did. In the end poor Johnny had to marry me. It was the way in those days, when a girl fell pregnant.

Now, in these new small hours, is Marie my daughter making the same mistake? My ears stretch into the dark house. But there are no — sounds.

I look again at the note. She'd left it on the kitchen table for me and I'd found it when I'd come in from the reunion with school-friends of yesteryear. It was beautifully written in her round neat hand, as usual.

'Hi Mum,' it said. 'I'm in. Hope you had a good time with

the Ancients. 2 Alkaseltzer below attached. Mike's staying the night in my room. I'll be leaving early for swimming practice — try not to waken you. Night, sleep well. XXX.'

'Now now, young man, you must get up and leave this house immediately. Never darken our door again.' Should I have marched into her room and delivered such a speech?

Or, at seventeen, was she now an adult, free to make her own choices, her own mistakes?

She had been my mistake. Not my only one, but the one with the farthest-reaching consequences.

I'd had a struggle to rear her after Johnny left home. We'd managed, with difficulty; I was always faced with the choice of going out to work and leaving her as a child alone in the house if she was ill or on holiday, or of staying at home and going without the low part-time wage that fed and clothed us and paid the rent. She'd been a difficult, resentful creature in her middle teens. But now she was an assured, hard-working, frank young woman.

So frank that I knew her views on religion — no such thing as God; politics — she was the last feather on the edge of the left-wing; and sex, no pill yet, but she'd start taking it when she thought it was time.

I, knotted with inhibition, gnarled with guilt on the subject of anything physical, had struggled to inform her on the bare facts of life. A book, tastefully coloured pink-for-girls, left lying around, had, I hoped, filled in the gaps. I hadn't been able to manage words like masturbation or penis.

Drink the tea. Calm streaking nerves. Turn on the radio softly to blank out thought. That's it, gentle music. Six chimes on the grandmother clock. He's still up there, that spiky-headed boy. In Marie's — bed? It would be utterly naive to imagine in these permissive days that he'd be anywhere else, wouldn't it? I must steel myself for the worst.

Marie had introduced him to me last December before the school Christmas party. Now he was in sixth year with her. He was just one of her large gang of friends. They'd usually spend Friday or Saturday evenings together in one or other of their family homes, playing music, dancing a little, talking, drinking lager. Often, when it was our turn, one or two of her girlfriends would stay the night; she'd do the same after an evening at theirs. Marie'd never mentioned this boy, Mike, particularly — or had I just not been listening?

Sometimes, as she rattled through all the minutiae of her day, or the night before's party, my mind would slide away

to dwell on some problem of my own — a bill I couldn't pay,
a lump I didn't want to notice in my breast.
Marie had her own life to live. With a bit of luck she'd
make a better job of hers than I had of mine. Things were
easier now, for a girl. She'd do well in her exams, perhaps get
into University to study Pharmacy. Her Saturday job in the
chemist would help her eke out her grant. She'd have a really
good career ahead of her, there would be no need to hunt for
some unreliable man to keep her. No need to hurry into
marriage. No need to marry at all? And children?
She was frank about children too. Couldn't abide them.
Said she for one wasn't going to add to the overpopulation of
the world and have her life eaten up by any puking, leaky brat.
But I remember how tenderly she loved her hard plastic, un-
responsive doll. She had a warm well of love to give, to someone, some day. Even though it was protected these days by
the thorns and pins of fashionable punkery.
Now I must find courage to go, must go treading up these
stairs, must go into her bedroom and stop, yes stop this spikey
Michael from doing any more, any further harm to my own,
my darling daughter.
Strong anger lights my way. Pink suede hushes my tread
on the stairs. Outside Marie's door I listen and feel like a
criminal.
Alarm bells scream. I back away, turn and run, weeping
hot tears down again to the kitchen. I wait, heart thumping.
Someone is coming, is coming downstairs. How will I face
him, them? There is a long yawn.
'Any tea left in the pot Mum?. What're you doing up so
early?'
She's wearing the worn-out pink kaftan she 'borrowed'
from me ages ago.
'Your note,' I mumble. 'Michael?'
'Oh he'll not want any tea. He's out for the count. Hope
you didn't mind — bunged him in the sleeping bag, he's so
thick he'll not feel the floor! I'll take him a coffee when I get
back from the baths, O.K.? Yuk this tea's cold — I'll make a
fresh pot. You look awful. Must've been quite a party! The
Ancients all still surviving? Oh, Jenny and I are going to
watch the rugger this morning at ten — Mike's playing for the
first, and Andy and Jim. Then we're all going back to Jenny's
tonight ... '
The kettle whistles. Outside the sun is beginning to rise.
A blackbird sings on the clothes pole.

ALONE ON THE CONTINENT

The farmhouse stood at the edge of the forest, its broad roofed buildings set around a stone courtyard. In front, the meadow dropped steeply to the railway bridge across the river to the red-tiled town.

Stormy weather came in from the east, rolling across the Bormerwald with a feeling of vastness and endless woods. Warm, hazy days followed, nothing moving but the silent hawks, not a sound through the late summer wildgrass. Restless weather, apprehensive somehow, with its mood always changing.

The place was like him. Jacob liked being there. Going up the forest path, cutting, carrying, stacking the firewood, the walks were journeys and the jobs weren't work, but ways to stay in the hard, strong place. Germany had a fascination for him, something ordered and deep in the light rush of Europe. Even the clouds seemed greater there, holding low on the border of the grave, shining land. Quiet morning after morning brightened his window. 'Write. The time is clear,' he said.

He had come alone from Greece six months ago. She had taken the children to friends in Scotland. From there, they would go back to Maine. It was the first truth he had ever known, their long apartness and now its fact. His life had fallen free like a wish. He had never imagined how much he missed it.

Yet at twilight sometimes he still felt her waiting. The wind brought the childrens' excited voices through the barn and sagging sheds. He answered them, he was so sure they were speaking. Was living there a stubbornness, a selfish mistake? The nights were empty, nobody's nights, still too near the time before.

Then one day in September, came a frayed blue letter covered with writing and half-penny stamps, even on the back and around the corners.

Molly had a friend and his name was Angus. She had a good swing and a puppy too. There was a drawing of their

cottage with an orange sun above it, and ducks on a pond with
pink and blue flowers. As for Moon, he guessed life was being
all right. He played his fiddle. It was too rainy for walking.
Then Jacob read her typed note twice. She would send
the children by train in two weeks. Please cable her if incon-
venient.
> I shall want them back with me for Christmas.
> I will post the times and tickets later. I hope
> you'll have a happy visit because it may be a
> while until the next. Father has found us a
> farm near Portland. I long to be in New Eng-
> land again.

'*Na, ja — ganz frisch hieroben!*' The postman watched
him with his hearty, cold eyes. The birches bent and flung
their sparrows, a few coloured leaves ticked across the slate
roof.

'My children are coming,' Jacob said. He pulled a straw
mattress into his workroom, then a Cretan wool rug, warm,
dark red. Simple and pretty, but still not enough. He added a
bench beside his table. He brought two candles and a sea shell
box, and a one-handed pocket watch he'd found in the forest.
He hung it on a nail for Moon and it started to run, an ikon
of time, with its little hurt face.

One day, he saw some kittens on the boundary wall.
They squirted away between the stones, all but a lazy, foolish
one who stretched and yawned with a noiseless mew. He put
it in his pocket: Molly's pet. It lived in the woodbin in the
waiting peace, and the tall days passed as he wrote by the
stove.

The Sunday came like any other, and he went down to
meet them at the station in Zwiesal. He stopped on the bridge
and some woodcutters passed him. He looked at the yellow-
tipped leaves in the water. Jacob did not have the gift of first-
feelings. They only came later, softer, slowly. Instead, he was
thinking of the day he'd left Tilos. The goats and gagged
chickens were ready in the boat: 'Travellers next!' the captain
called out. He remembered her wrapped in her sheepskin coat,
rigid and sure at the end of the pier. They too would be
leaving soon, she said. They would meet again, after some
time. And then it happened — their lives grew smaller, tilted
and sank in the rough March waves. He relaxed with the hurt
and the rightness of the journey on. He thought of the book
and the long summer elsewhere.

Jacob was the only one on the platform, as the train

eased past him, slowed and stopped with Molly's wild face
and Moon smiling calmly. 'What if I'd missed them?' he
thought.

The boy was taller, moving loosely, sure of himself.
Molly's hair was down to her waist. Six months in her life: it
could be everything. The time had been longer, far longer
than it seemed. They told all their news before they left town,
Molly hanging on his arm and Moon walking backwards,
building up stories. It frightened him, how much they needed
to say, the blind, telling need of them. They ran before him
with their knapsacks on their heads, up the clay road and
across the meadow, finally bolting in a panic to claim the cat
and their room in the high, autumn place.

Jacob looked at them bumbling on ahead, still shouting
in their strange, shrill voices. Were they really here because of
him? It seemed there should be some larger event. Yet maybe
he loved them more than he knew, a wordless love always inside him. He felt the miles of distance they'd come, and the
shy half-reach from her, obliged, uncertain.

He washed their clothes instead of chopping. And when
the wood ran out, he let them break up his table. They fell
on it like savages with stones and an axe and pulled it to
pieces in the seed-flecked mud. Soon their clothes, all of
them, were dirty again, but the kitchen was too, so why did
it matter?

He couldn't continue the book and resume his old life
also, but both were done — remarkable, really. Impossible,
writing with such noise in the hall, unlikely to think under
these conditions. And yet somehow it happened that way.
Molly came in with her blackberry hands, took his typewriter
paper, scribbled and drew. Moon lay dreaming with his head
on his arm. No sounds but the kitten and the rain on the windows. 'We're getting older and quieter, Jacob.' Jacob looked
up and saw it was true. For minutes on end, they were silent
together.

Soon winter hung about the place, also his first winter
there. It was only October and the snowflakes were falling.
One dim afternoon, the cows came down the forest path,
ringing lower and fainter through the meadowgrass gate, and
red autumn flew up and blew along with them. He stood outside in the dripping quiet. It amazed him that he was half-
way through his life. It was deeper, like falling, the stillness
ahead.

Then Moon cuts his leg and shouts to a scream, flings the chopper against the bulging tin lean-to. What a noise out there now, all of a sudden. A white owl opens both eyes on a fencepost, and the hungry sparrows fly up in a fright. Jacob quickly rights things — he ties on a bandage and starts the tea early. Then Molly squelches in, wholly caked with manure, even her tongue and her filled-up ears — stands growling like an ogre with her arms held out. Jacob readies a bath, but no hot water. This is because there's no wood for the fire, or dry clothes to wear to go out and fetch some. The crazy blur of backwards progressions stretches to a lumpy time of its own, with its own curt language and peculiar events.

'Take it, why don't you?' Moon looks away and rolls his eyes. Checkers with Molly, hopeless, really.

'Moon's games are draggy 'cause you have to do things.' Molly, like Jacob, can't move one direction, only on the squares in this same, slanting way. The hand-drawn board, the brown and white road-stones — Molly just shrugs at the dull, ordered space of it.

'She hasn't got the wits.' Moon sighs sadly, dreaming Moon from life's other side.

'Or she's got too many.' Jacob turns a page.

'Whatever she's got, it's no use to me. I'm walking down to the shops again.'

'In the snow?' quacks his sister, standing on her head.

'Aye,' is all he says. 'Not much company about. I'm wanting my mates.' And he goes out in a blizzard. Molly asks for some more to eat. A bird in the woods: it's the first time they've heard one.

'Who are you?' Jacob wondered sometimes. 'Where are you going, little changed lives?' He watched them stumbling through the snow-patched meadow, crossing and colliding with their dragon kites, pushing each other back home, still hungry.

Then a string of fine days, a week of bright weather. The hawks circled slowly by the castle on the hill, and the white clouds plumed and grew in the distance — chariots, islands, come-apart faces. Moon watched them from the window with his chin in his hands, solitary Moon, with his dusty fiddle. Jacob hardly remembered the time before him, and yet they'd never met somehow.

'There's nothing to do at Jacob's house.'

Jacob came in and that's what Moon said.

Here at Jacob's, with the crows in the yellow weeds at

the doorway. He had arrived here on a Sunday himself, walked up to the lost-looking place from the highroad and lit a twig fire to warm his hands. He rested for some days, and no one minded — he found the owner and the owner shrugged, 'Stay.' So he lived there, but lightly. He couldn't go back to America now. No, not another year of wishful coast walks, with his novel unwritten and his life come free.

And so he remained at Jacob's House. Here it was with Jacob in it: the invisible, funless place he preferred, and what he'd come up with, exactly. It was like an old photograph, a poor part assigned to him — Jacob on the continent, visited by his children, high in the woodlands with nothing to do. How sensible his children made him!

The weekly torment of Molly's bath was well beyond his mirth and patience. 'Nothing's good in this shabby place! *Kuzulo! Grinyaro!* I don't want to stay here anymore, Jacob!'

Crazy man, cross man. She hit him with her hand. Now, what was this trouble and how had it happened that this sun-born child was shrieking and stamping, calling him names and *kuzulo*? Jacob asked her: 'How is it you know me so well, to flood my floor and slap me like this?' She laughed, but his anxious daughter was beside herself, with her beads and her hair mashed flat in a tangle, and she couldn't love him or see anymore.

What had become of his wild, Greek children, hanging from the fig trees, eating grapes on the beach? He remembered the cooing white doves on the rooftops, the pink almond blossoms, the coffee-house chat. There was no one on the hills of rocky, walled fields. The sea gales lashed through the bamboo windbreaks and turned the ledges of olive trees silver. He found her by the sluiceway behind the house and told her of the other woman. She covered her ears and couldn't hear him. He had looked at her broken face and thought, 'This is mine also. A sadness is coming.'

'Old Jacob's going to have his peace back soon,' Moon smiled as he whittled a chestnut stick with the white chips sailing over his shoulder, and the kitten catching them one by one.

'Jacob! Hee! Hee! Have you seen what Moon's making?'

Jacob listened to the lapping gully stream. Their voices were like thoughts of them, fading absent.

'It looks like his — you know! Let's see! It does!'

'Let *go*, Molly! There, you silly bugger!'

'Oh, Jacob! Now Moon's hit me with it!'

A smack and a thud — extreme little beings rolling over themselves, struggling out of breath, sleeping where they stopped with their heads on their books and their feet on the wall by the spluttering lantern. How were they his? They were no one's children on their way somewhere. The mixed memories of them could be so serious, their lives cut with journeys between him and her.

They took a picnic round the skirt of the hill and spent all the sunshine choosing a place, while the gully stream laughed and dropped down lightly. Jacob wondered at their hurry to always have more.

They took a walk to Falkenstein Castle. It hung from the ridge like an old yellow tooth. Moon made for the tower, directly, but Molly stayed close to him, held his leg, even. How would she see him some day, Jacon wondered. A tall man who took her to a frightening place, who drew her to him and made her see it?

He bought them a calendar with coloured windows. Each day had a saint and a story inside it. They opened them all, backwards, any-way, till December lay bare to its bright little birth. The bells in the valley rang every day now. The first heavy snow fell slowly with sureness. A pause and a difference hushed around them. Then just as he'd imagined, the post-man cycled into the courtyard, pipping his horn and smiling like fate with a sprig of holly behind his ear.

The letter was from Galloway, registered, numbered, certain to find him. A time-table, two tickets and a twenty pound note.

> They will be sad to leave you, I know. But
> school starts soon and there is much to be
> done before the flight. You see, next year
> will challenge us all.

'But where will you be? Are you staying here, Jacob?' Molly asked him, clean and fresh.

'Yes,' he said. He could feel the miles they were going, and the final, double-distance of sea.

They waited beside him at the end of the platform, with their bags bursting open and their shoes untied. The train crossed the valley and clattered through the poplars to the trestle bridge with a burst of brakes and a screeching *hoo!* There was a sharpness like a panic, choiceless, new, and this was its moment and its warning come true. A surprise of understanding held close around them. Then all at once his children were gone.

The clock struck one. It was a sunny, snow-smudged day, the yellow quilts airing from the open windows and the woodsmoke hanging in an even layer. A milk wagon rattled along the brick street. Two chimney-sweeps swore and parted around him, staring back white-eyed from under their hats. He passed the last houses of tidy families, each with its garden and its lineful of clothes. A cartload of foresters rocked past the crossroads, eating their lunches with their boots hanging down, laughing and calling in dialect. Then once again, and again a surprise, the perfect gift of stillness and order.

Jacob swept the room as best he could. There were pyramids and slides of random rubbish, trails of drawings and open pens. A puzzled kitten, a pink paper saint — a stopped watch, a whistle, three wee rubber wheels. Spent things, leftover, wasted somehow. It was all he could give them, apart from himself.

He looked at the day of rabbits running. The sun came under the drifted woods and lit up a fox in the spots of birch leaves. Then the fern tops by the fence jumped alive in the light, and along the border of drooping brambles. He walked to the stile in the bright, clear evening. The violet mountains rose over the clouds, islands of a greater land ahead in the dark.

ROBERT CRAWFORD

DUNOON

Mist becomes polythene we burst with our fingers.
Along the coastline hills are wrapped up.
Tomatoes, leeks. The country is on a level
With these things. Tugging our cold thumbs,

Petulantly pleading, love
Cannot replace shopping or the mending of telephones.
Accelerating away behind tinted windows,
The chairman drafts a long letter.

DOOR

All day our hyacinths grew in the dark
Cupboard which had been the school's first door.
We hung our coats on petrified iron pegs
In the stonefloored cloakroom, hoping the bulbs would
    flower

That coming year in bowls which had our names
Feltpenned beneath. Nearer the time, their scent
Entered our anoraks. We wore it home
Smugly aware of everything it meant:

More life set out on Miss Wood's nature table.
After Ann Gibson died, who'd smelt of piss,
Our class pooled money so we could buy flowers
And send them to her like a guilty kiss

Given by boys who hated girls, and girls
Who cried in the classroom, crayoning in newsbooks
A small white ambulance. We danced that week
Through the wooden gym like hyacinth-scented spooks

To fast piano. Till one day Miss Wood
Opened the cupboard and came out with showers
Of sneezing pink. This bowl was mine, its peat
Damp to my thumb. I carried home these flowers,

Mum set them on the wireless. Every morning
At breakfast time their teastained odour poured
Over the news a sniffed-at rising sun
Grown in the dark behind our school's first door.

THE SCOTTISH NATIONAL CUSHION SURVEY

Our heritage of Scottish cushions is dying.
Teams of careful young people on training schemes
Arrived through a government incentive, counting
Every cushion. In Saltcoats, through frosty Lanark.
They even searched round Callanish
For any they'd missed. There are no more Scottish cushions
Lamented the papers. Photographs appeared
Of the last cushion found in Gaeldom.
Silk cushions, pin cushions, pulpit cushions.
We must preserve our inheritance.
So the museums were built: The Palace of Cushions, the
    National
Museum of Soft Seating, and life went on elsewhere
Outside Scotland. The final Addendum was published
Of *Omnes Pulvini Caledonii.*
Drama documentaries. A chapter closed.
And silently in Glasgow quick hands began
Angrily making cushions.

NOTES ON CONTRIBUTORS

MOIRA BURGESS, born in Cambeltown in 1936, is a full-time writer and mother. She received a Scottish Arts Council writer's bursary in 1982. Publications include *The Day Before Tomorrow* (novel, 1971); *The Glasgow novel, a bibliography* (1972, 2nd edition forthcoming); *Streets of Stone* (Salamander Press 1985; anthology of Glasgow short stories, edited with Hamish Whyte); and short stories in *NWS 2*, *Scottish Short Stories* 1985, and *Original Prints* (Polygon 1985).

ROBERT CRAWFORD was born in 1959 in Glasgow. A graduate of Glasgow and Oxford, he is now a Research Fellow at St. Hugh's College, Oxford. His poems have appeared in *Gairfish*, *Glasgow Magazine*, in both the previous issues of *NWS*, *PN Review*, *Poetry Review*, and on Radio 3. He is co-editor of *Verse*, and co-author (with W. N. Herbert) of *Sterts & Stobies, Poems in Scots* (1985).

PAT GERBER, itinerant Glaswegian since 1934, survived school, married, mothered and matured. Langside College gave her Highers. After struggling through an Honours M.A., the fifth baby and divorce she worked in Further Education. Then Cyril Gerber kindly married her and encouraged her to 'work' less and write more. These stories are her first published works of fiction. She is currently working on an M. Litt. and a novel.

VALERIE GILLIES was born in Alberta, Canada, 1948, brought up in Scotland, on the Lanarkshire moors, and educated at the universities of Edinburgh and Mysore, South India. She is now a poet and freelance writer living in Edinburgh. Her publications include *Trio: New Poets from Edinburgh* (New Rivers Press); *Each Bright Eye* (Canongate); and *Bed of Stone* (Canongate). She was a contributor to *NWS 2*.

STANLEY ROGER GREEN was born in Edinburgh not too recently. Schooled variously in Edinburgh and Clackmannanshire, he was sidetracked into Leith Nautical College before completing formal education at Edinburgh College of Art as an architect. He has travelled widely as cadet seaman, soldier, student and architect. Author of about ninety poems, one of which appeared in *NWS 2*, and as many short stories plus about twenty-odd broadcast items, his first collection of poetry, *A Suburb of Belsen* (Paul Harris) came out in 1977. Four plays have been performed by Edinburgh Theatre Workshop companies.

ANDREW GREIG was born in Bannockburn in 1951 and grew up in Anstruther. He took first class honours in philosophy at Edinburgh University, has had various jobs, and now makes a living, just, from writing. He was writer in residence at Glasgow University 1979-81, and was the Scottish/Canadian exchange fellow 1982-3. He climbed with the 1985 Pilkington Everest Expedition. His publications are *White Boats* (1972), *Men on Ice* (1977), *Surviving Passages* (1982) and *Summit Fever* (1985).

RODERICK HART was born in Aberdeenshire in 1944 but grew up in St Andrews. A graduate of Aberdeen University, he is now a lecturer in Communication at Telford College, Edinburgh. His work has previously appeared in magazines, *The Scotsman*, two anthologies of Scottish verse, and in *NWS* in 1983.

DAVID KINLOCH was born in Lennoxtown in 1959 and has spent most of his life in Glasgow, graduating from Glasgow University in 1982. He was a Snell Exhibitioner at Balliol College, Oxford, researching in French literature, and has just been appointed to the Bourne Junior Research Fellowship at St Anne's College, Oxford. He is co-editor of *Verse*, and was a contributor to *NWS* in 1983.

NORMAN KREITMAN is a doctor who has a research post in Edinburgh where he has lived for many years. His work has appeared in various magazines and anthologies. The publication of his first book *Touching Rock* is currently being negotiated, and a second collection is approaching completion.

ROBBIE KYDD was born in 1918. A retired social work teacher, he is writing a sequence of stories, each exploring one of the eight 'critical periods of development' in the human life-cycle as identified by Erik H. Erikson. 'Auld Zimmery', published in *NWS* 2, and the two printed here are 'work in progress' from the sequence.

BRIAN McCABE was born in 1951 in Edinburgh, where he now lives. He has published three collections of poetry, the most recent of which *Spring's Witch* (Mariscat Press, 1984) won a Scottish Arts Council Book Award. His first collection of short stories *The Lipstick Circus* was published this year by Mainstream. He has lived as a freelance writer since 1980 and is presently the Writer in Residence for Stirling District Council. He contributed to both *NWS* 1 and 2.

MAUREEN MACNAUGHTAN was born in Glasgow in 1945. She served in the WRAF, has travelled widely and now lives in Moray where she is the President of the Moray and Nairn Writers' Workshop. She has been published in *Success Anthology* and will be represented in a new anthology for Scottish primary schools.

DEBORAH MOFFATT was born in Vermont in 1953 and now lives in Auchtermuchty. At eighteen she began to travel and lived in several Latin American countries before settling in Scotland. She has worked as a journalist and as a Middle Eastern dancer. Her poems have appeared in Scottish and American journals.

IAN MORRISON is a graduate of Aberdeen University in English and Scottish Literature, and this is his first published story. He was born in Torphins in 1963. His father worked on farms around Strachan till 1971 when his family moved to Arbuthnott. They moved again to their present address just outside Laurencekirk three years later.

WILMA MURRAY was born in 1939 near Inverurie. She was educated at Inverurie Academy and Aberdeen University. She taught in schools for several years before joining Aberdeen College of Education as a lecturer in Geography. This year stories appear in *Cencrastus, Chapman* and in an anthology of Scottish women writers. She was a contributor to *NWS* 2.

ROLAND PORTCHMOUTH was born in London in 1923. He served in the Royal Navy 1942-6 and was an art teacher and lecturer in teacher training colleges 1951-68. He is the author of art books and of a children's novel. Religious paintings by him are permanently mounted in Peebles Old Parish Church and poems are regularly published in *Life and Work*. He is a Church of Scotland minister in Perthshire.

IAN RANKIN was born in Cardenden, Fife in 1960. In 1983 he was runner-up in *The Scotsman* Short Story Competition. In 1984 he won the Radio Forth Short Story Competition. His stories have been published in *The Scotsman, New Edinburgh Review, Cencrastus* and *Scottish Review*, and broadcast on Radio Forth and BBC Radio Four. His first novel *The Flood* will be published by Polygon Books in 1986.

GILLEAN SOMERVILLE was born in Glasgow and grew up Edinburgh. She has taught English in Marseilles and Cheltenham, been a secretary in London and an administrator in the Universities of Strathclyde and Stirling. She has been a regular contributor to *NWS* since her first published story appeared there in 1983 and has had other stories accepted by *The Scottish Review* and *Chapman*.

JAMES C. Q. STEWART was born in Dundee in 1952, and has lived in Brechin, Arbroath, and the Cupar area. He graduated from Dundee in 1984, and is doing postgraduate work on Virginia Woolf at Edinburgh. Individual poems have appeared in *Gallimaufry*. Six poems appeared last year in *Seagate II*.

VALERIE THORNTON was born in 1954. She went to school in Stirling and returned to Glasgow in 1972. Her stories and poems have appeared in *NWS* 1 and 2, and in *Streets of Stone; Lines Review* has accepted five poems. Articles ranging from cockroaches to hallmarking have also appeared in diverse magazines.

JACKSON WEBB was born in 1940, and has lived in Scotland for the past 14 years. Stories by him have appeared in Scottish Arts Council anthologies, *Blackwoods, Words, Cornhill, Scottish Review* and on Radio 3. His first novel, *The Last Lemon Grove* was chosen by George Mackay Brown as *The Scotsman*'s Book of the Year. He has received the Tom Gallon Award, a Scottish Arts Council bursary in 1980, and the Scottish Conservation Society's Award for Regional Fiction. He was Writer in Residence for Yorkshire Arts (Richmond) in 1983-4, and contributed to *NWS* 1 and 2.

ESTHER WOOLFSON was born and brought up in Glasgow and attended the universities of Jerusalem and Edinburgh where she studied Chinese. She has travelled widely in the Middle East and has worked intermittently as a translator from Hebrew. She now lives in reluctant, and she hopes temporary exile, in London.